This book is dedicated to

Nalin Lee Ratpinyotip Scott

Acknowledgments

I would like to thank and pay my respect to my son, Neran J. P. Weaver for giving me inspiration to write this book when he become a novice monk during summer school holiday.

I also would like to thank Anthony, Sean and Japer, for attending the Summer Novice Monks Training Course and give me a lot of their opinion and ideas in this book.

A special thanks to J. P. Darby for being a part of our family and join the novice monk ceremony.

Many Thanks to my family in Thailand for always believe in me.

I would like to thank Dr Paul M Weaver for all support both mentality and physicality during this summer training period.

Ocean Thanks to any volunteer, who help do many jobs includes cooking, gardening, services and anything in the Buddhapadipa Temple.

Finally, I would like to thank: Rung Ratpinyotip Scott, Brian and Taravali Jackson, Ryan Jennings, Kalenza Prayuenyong, Jaruvan Mcwong, Dr. Sirilaksana Kunjara, Nongnat Broughton and family for their financial support to write this book.

When My Son Becomes

NOVICE

MONK

in United Kingdom

Dr Kesorn Pechrach Weaver

When My Son Becomes

NOVICE

MONK

in United Kingdom

Dr Kesorn Pechrach Weaver

Pechrach Publishing

When My Son Becomes Novice Monk in United Kingdom

By Dr Kesorn Pechrach Weaver

ISBN 978-0-9931178-8-6

PECHRACH PUBLISHING

7 Boundary Road, Bishops Stortford, Hertfordshire, CM23 5LE, England, United Kingdom. Tel: (+44) 1279 508020, +44 (0) 7443426937

Published 20148by Pechrach Publishing

Illustrations @ Paul M Weaver, P Nirut, Patcharaphol Pongvijit

Message from Author

The author has no intention to write any book during this summer. However, after spending time in the Buddahapadipa for many days. There are many things give me some inspiration to write a story about the novice monks in the United Kingdom. From from dawn until dark, I have observed the way that the novice monks live and do the activity.

I also have a chance to talk and ask some questions about the life of the novice monks in the UK with Mrs. Rung Scott, while she was cleaning the leaves in the forest behind the temple. She told me her son, Nalin Scott, was a novice monk in the Wat Buddhapadipa when he was young. Thus, she can give me very useful suggestion.

Furthermore, there is some people misunderstand about the novice monks. They may think if a boy has their head shaved and wear a yellow clothes, then he is a novice monk. This book will show them that they are wrong.

Dr. Kesorn P Weaver

22nd September 2018

United Kingdom

Table of Contents

Table of Figures

robes

monks

CHAPTER 1

Buddhapadipa Temple

July 2018 after the school ends and the Tennis Wimbledon 2018 is finished, the summer holiday has started. Our son is going to move from primary school to secondary school. It is a big change for him since he had studied in that school for eight years since nursery until year 6. The transition process between the two schools have done before the end of the summer term.

However, we can feel that it would not be easy for him such as big changes, not only the environment but also the teachers and the school system.

As a mother and a Buddhist, my experience of practise meditation. I have known that the meditation would help my son to deal with the changing situation and cope with the changing. Not only in his secondary school, but be a teenage in the near future for him. Therefore, we try to find out where and how he can learn basic and a place where he practice of meditating. In the safe environment, the teacher can teach the meditation methodology in English and the important thing is the place must not be very far from us to make a visit from time to time.

Our base location is half way between Cambridge and London. Therefore, everything around 50 miles is acceptable for travelling.

Figure 1.1: Wat Buddhapadipa

It is a six weeks summer holiday in the United Kingdom, we have two options:

1st Option: We will travel to Thailand, where some of my Thai family still lives there. However, there are some concern about the communication. Our son neither speak nor understand Thai language very well. Thus, it would be very difficult for him to learn and understand the methods of meditation properly. In addition, the very hot and humid weather in Thailand could have some effect on learning methodology.

Figure 1.2: Front gate Wat Buddhapadipa

2nd Option: The learning and Practise place must be in the United Kingdom, where most people can speak English very well. He will familiar with the weather as well as the environment. However, how can we find this course in this country?

Luckily we are in the year 2018: Internet of Things. We start searching for the meditation course for kids via the internet.

There are information about the summer Samanera training course at the webpage http://www.padipa.org/ and http://www.watbuddhapadipa.org

Figure 1.3: Wat Buddhapadipa fence

We find out that between 4th August 2018 and 12th August 2018, the Buddhapadipa Temple, Wimbledon, London, has a program for ordination of Novices Monks or as known as the Summer Samanera Training Course, which they held the event every year during the summer holiday. We think it is a good opportunity for our son to learn about the Buddhist and the way that the monks live, including learning meditation at the same time.

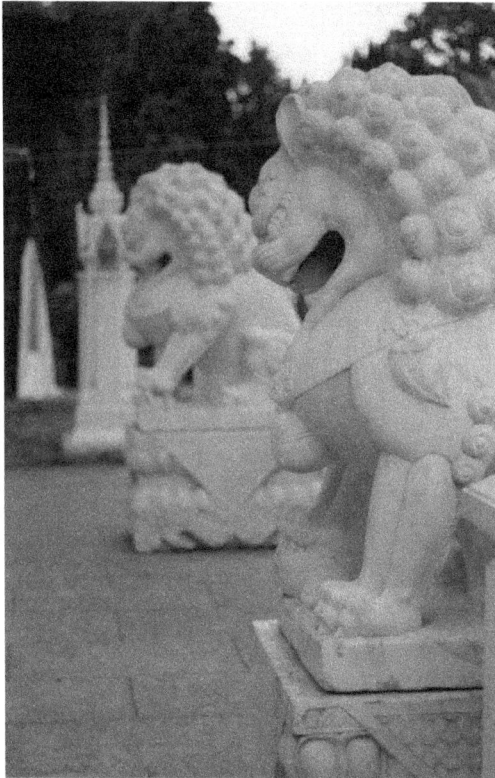

Figure 1.4: Entrace to the Uposatha Hall

On Sunday 15th July 2018 we make a telephone call at the number +44 (0) 208 946 1357 to find out more information about the Summer Samanera and make an appointment for visiting the temple.

We know it is not easy for us to drive direct pass the centre of London, United Kingdom. There are many congestion zones and low carbon emission zones to pay for the charge.

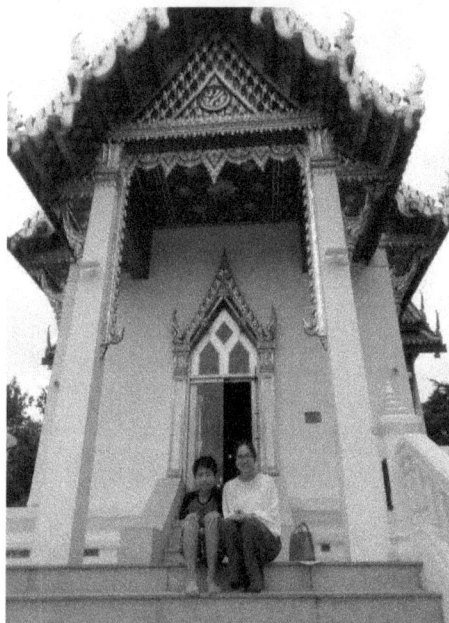

Figure 1.5: Visiting the Buddhapadipa

The lady, who pick the phone is very kind, her name is Dor Mai, It is a Thai name and it translates to English as flowers. Then, she forwards our call to the monk, who provide us more information about this course.

On Sunday 22nd July 2018, we start our journey from our base via Motorway M11, M25, M4, and many roads in the centre of London as the Satlelight Navigation leads us to our destination. It takes us just over three long hot and sweating hours in the traffic jam, roads under construction and diversion.

Figure 1.6: Fence around the Uposatha Hall

However, as soon as our car turn and drive pass the temple gate. We can feel just like we are in a different world, quiet, peaceful and happy.

The Uposatha hall building is very beautiful and there is the same plan as the Buddhists Wat in Thailand. The layout and the set up is the standard with a white concrete fence around the building.

There are four stair entrances to the upper level, which fence up around the top of the Uposatha Hall.

Figure 1.7: Wat Buddhapadipa Architecture

The building with Wat Thai architecture standing in the middle of the big grass area next to the lake with there are various birds and ducks. It just likes we have got lost in the different world, not in the London, which is the capital of the United Kingdom. The most busy working lifestyle and the world capital of financing, which we just passed by less than a few minutes ago. The big plot of land and garden, there are a pond and forest in the same area. It is like a real museum and the temple in the same place.

Figure 1.8: Bell tower building next to the lake

The Bell tower building was painted with red colour standing beside the lake next to the main building, which used as head office and a place where all of the monks stay.

Figure 1.9: Wild ducks in the forest

Figure 1.10: The pond next to the main building

CHAPTER 2

Application

After we have walked around the green area and have done some survey overall building and lake inside the boundary of the Wat Buddhapadipa.

Figure 2.1: Uposatha Hall

We just learn that they have some activities such as the teaching Thai language, Thai culture and Thai dancing for children on Sunday every weekend. It calls Sunday school.

Figure 2.2: Sunday school

We walk into the main building and inform them about our purpose of visiting and we would like to have more information about the Summer Samanera Training Course.

The Course director and Senior Teacher Monk, PM Bhatsakorn, kindly explain the procedure, term and condition including some requirement. The most two important things that concern for us are:

1) Our son has to have his head shaved

2) He will not allow to eat dinner

Figure 2.3: Buddha inside the main building

However, PM Bhatsakorn explains to us that our son will not be starving. He will have breakfast and big portion of lunch, which it is the main meal of the day. Also, he will allow to have some liquid, and juice drinks in the afternoon and evening. It calls "Pana"

Parents Questions

We have many questions includes where he will sleep, Where he will eat, can he access to water or drink any times, what kinds of clothes he has to pack, can he pack sleeping bag to sleep here and can he bring his mobile phone.

We have been showing the places he will sleep and eat. About his cloth, most of the time during he is a Samanera status, he will wear the yellow robe all the time. Therefore, he just needs to pack some underwear with him.

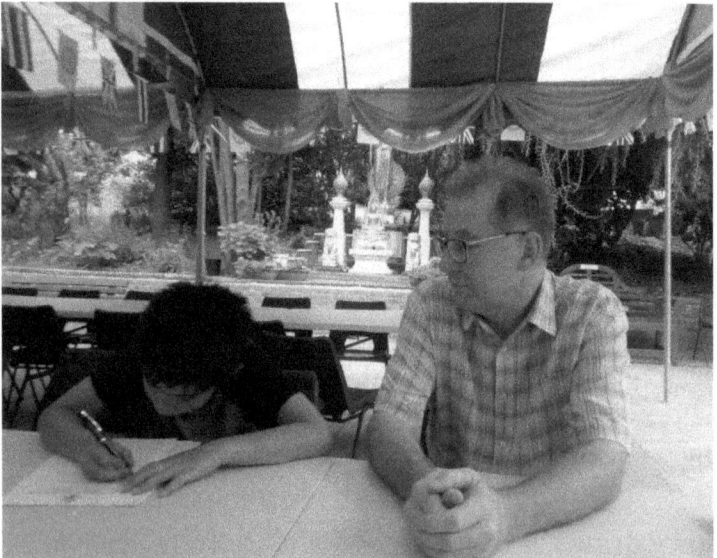

Figure 2.4: Filling the application form

For his bed, he can pack his own sleeping bag with his own pillow and a duvet set which he uses at home. It does not need to be the yellow colour because it is not easy to find the whole bed set in yellow colour like the monk's yellow robe colour in the United Kingdom.

PM Bhatsakorn answers every question clearly and make sure that the parents clearly understand on every point and happy for all the answers.

Not only we as parents are happy, but also our son has to make a commitment as well. Our son has some questions to ask PM Bhatsakorn and when he is happy to follow the term and condition, including the requirement that he has to practise ten precepts while he is in the Samanera status.

In addition, he has to practise at home in advance the reciting Pali passages requesting for ordination, which the ceremony will held on Sat 4th August 2018. PM Bhatsakorn gives us the YouTube links for practise at home https://youtu.be/_yCyDjqWIAA

When My Son Becomes Novice Monk in United Kingdom

CHAPTER 3

Arriving Day

We have been recommended that we should bring our son to the Wat Buddhapapdipa one day before the ordination of novice monk ceremony.
Therefore, we arrive on Friday 3rd August 2018 in the afternoon.

Figure 3.1: The main building

There are totally four children will attend this year 2018 summer novice monks training course. Tonight they will have a night's sleep in the main building.

Figure 3.2: The main building bedroom

Their parents who have to travel from far away like us, the monks allow us to sleep in the classroom in the Sunday school building, as shown in Figure 3.1

We take two days off from work on Friday 3rd August and on Monday 6th August 2018. We would like to make sure that our son is settled in a new environment and familiar with the teacher monks in the Buddahapadipa temple.

There are two boys arrive earlier than us, their name is, Anthony 12 years old and Japer 8 years old. Since they are the same age, thus they get along and be friends immediately.

Figure 3.3: The Sunday school building

We pack some pillow, blanket and sleeping bags, including some water and fruits. We know that the main gate will be closed in the evening. Therefore, it is not a good idea to go out for our dinner. We just have fruits for dinner. The weather in August is very hot, the temperature rises up to 36 degree C in London.

However, as we have known the English weather always changing. It will be rain, cold and warm in the same day. Therefore, we pack both thin and thick clothes. After we have a key and unpack, we walk around the temple area to survey some forest and a pond behind the main building.

Figure 3.4: The inner main gate

Figure 3.5: The outer main gate

The Wat Buddhapadipa has a high fence around the temple area and also it has two gates before people can get in the temple area. Therefore, it is pretty safe for our son to stay here. Furthermore, the outer and inner gate will be closed at 6 PM and re-open again in the morning at 9 AM.

The facilities building block includes showers and toilets are available at the far end.

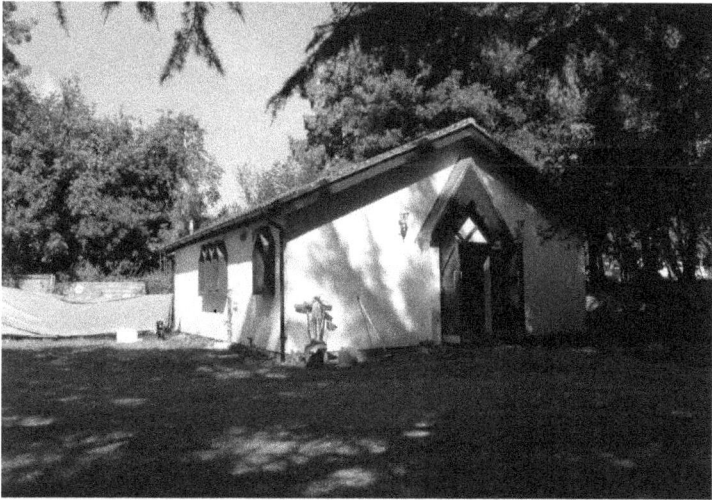

Figure 3.6: The toilet building

There are clearly separated between man and woman toilets. There is also a temporary line to dry the laundry behind the blue fence behind to the toilet block. There are many wash basins and toilets. There are three shower rooms.

Figure 3.7: Inside the toilet building

Figure 3.8: The shower room

CHAPTER 4

Pali Preparing

We have known in advance that our son has to practise the reciting Pali passages requesting for ordination.

Figure 4.1: New Samanera candidates

However, on the day that we arrived on Fri 3rd August 2018, Pra Nirut, who is the teacher monk and act as the mentor for these new novice monks. He gathers them to practise Pali Recite in the park next to the Uposatha Hall. He also explains the ordination procedure for novice monks to the Samanera candidates in details.

Figure 4.2: Pra Nirut

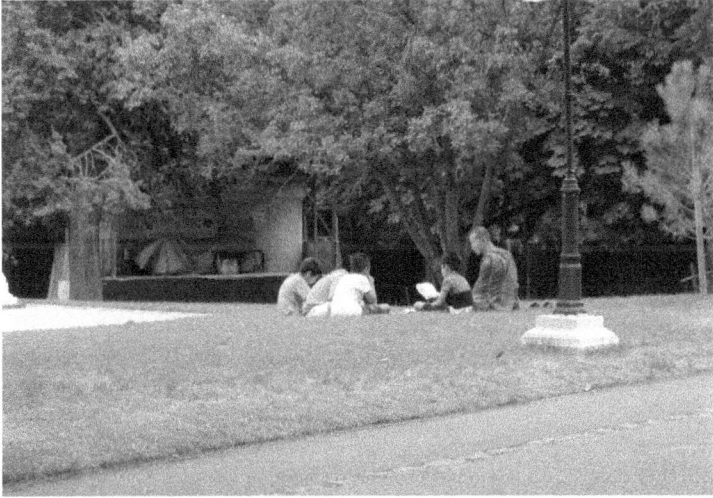

Figure 4.3: Practise Pali in the afternoon

The Pali Recitation for Novice Monks' Ordination was recorded by Phramaha Bhatsakorn Piyobhaso and available on YouTube as linked below: https://www.youtube.com/watch?v=_yCyDjqWIAA &feature=youtu.be

The Pali passages were written in English pronunciation. My son spends couple weeks listen and read out loud along with the video. However, it is not easy for him to remember since it is a difficult language to learn. Although, I myself who have familiar with some of the sound, still find it is not easy to copy the sound and remember the Pali word.

All candidates say together:

Ete mayaṁ bhante sucira- parinibbutampi, taṁ bhagavantaṁ saraṇaṁ gacchāma, dhammaññca bhikkhusaṇghaññca, labheyyāma mayaṁ bhante, tassa bhagavato dhammavinaye pabbajjaṁ.

Dutiyampi mayaṁ bhante sucira-parinibbutampi, taṁ bhagavantaṁ saraṇaṁ gacchāma, dhammaññca bhikkhusaṅghaññca, labheyyāma mayaṁ bhante, tassa bhagavato dhammavinaye pabbajjaṁ.

Tatiyampi mayaṁ bhante sucira-parinibbutampi, taṁ bhagavantaṁ saraṇaṁ gacchāma, dhammaññca bhikkhusaṇghaññca, labheyyāma mayaṁ bhante, tassa bhagavato dhammavinaye pabbajjaṁ.

Mayaṁ bhante pabbajjaṁ yācāma, imāni kāsāyāni vatthāni gahetvā, pabbājetha, no bhante, anukampaṁ upādāya.

Dutiyampi mayaṁ bhante pabbajjaṁ yācāma, imāni kāsāyāni vatthāni gahetvā, pabbājetha, no bhante, anukampaṁ upādāya.

Tatiyampi mayaṁ bhante pabbajjaṁ yācāma, imāni kāsāyāni vatthāni gahetvā, pabbājetha, no bhante, anukampaṁ upādāya.

Repeat this after the monk:

Kesā	Tacō
Lomā	Dantā
Nakhā	Nakhā
Dantā	Loma
Taco	Kesā

Requesting the refuges and precepts

Ahaṁ bhante saraṇasīlaṁ yācāmi,

Dutiyampi ahaṁ bhante saraṇasīlaṁ yācāmi

Tatiyampi ahaṁ bhante saraṇasīlaṁ yācāmi

Namo tassa bhagavato arahato sammā sambuddhassa

(repeat this after the monk 3 times)

The monk says: **Yamahaṁ vadāmi taṁ vadehi**

The candidate replies: **Āma bhante.**

Buddhaṁ saraṇaṁ gacchāmi.

Dhammaṁ saraṇaṁ gacchāmi.

Saṅghaṁ saraṇaṁ gacchāmi.

Dutiyampi buddhaṁ saraṇaṁ gacchāmi.
Dutiyampi dhammaṁ saraṇaṁ gacchāmi.
Dutiyampi saṅghaṁ saraṇaṁ gacchāmi.

Tatiyampi buddhaṁ saraṇaṁ gacchāmi.
Tatiyampi dhammaṃ saraṇaṃ gacchāmi.
Tatiyampi saṅghaṁ saraṇaṁ gacchāmi.

The monk says: **Tisaraṇa gamanaṃ nitthitaṃ**
Answer: **Āma bhante**

Repeat after the monk sentence by sentence:

Pāṇātipātā veramaṇī
Adinnādānā veramaṇī
Abrahmacariyā veramaṇī
Musāvādā veramaṇī
Suramerayamajjapamādatthānā veramaṇī

Vikāla bhojanā veramaṇī
Naccagīta-vāditavisūka-dassanā-veramaṇī
**Mālāgandha-vilepana-dhāraṇa-maṇḍana-
vibhūsanaṭṭhānā-veramaṇī**
Uccāsayana-mahāsayanā-veramaṇī
Jātarūpa-rajata-patiggahaṇā-veramaṇī

Imāni dasa sikkhāpadāni samādiyāmi
(repeat this 3 times)

Figure 4.4: Pali Recitation for Novice Monks

In the evening on that day, the Samanera candidates join the evening chanting with the group of teacher monks. This will help them to familiar with the evening chanting activity, which will be their routine later on.

Figure 4.5: Practise Evening chanting

Furthermore, Pra Nirut leads them to practise the Pali Recitation for Novice Monks' Ordination one more time before going to bed. He tries to practise with them as often as possible since they do not have a lot of time to prepare. This practise Pali procedure in Thailand may take up to a month that require the Samanera candidate to live and stay in the temple before the Ordination ceremony day.

What the Samanera candidate in the United Kingdom can do is only practise in the morning after the morning chanting finish before they join the hair cutting ceremony, which schedule after lunch time.

Figure 4.6: Practise Pali Recitation for Novice Monks

Since the Samanera candidates do not have a lot of time to practise the Pali message in their home. Some of them just finish their school in the summer term. Thus, they need to arrive at the temple at least one day before the ceremony day. The purpose of this is for them to practise in the morning after morning chanting.

CHAPTER 5

Morning on the day

Figure 5.1: Early morning inside the temple

Since we arrived yesterday afternoon and sleep over at the school. Therefore, we can get up early and walk around the temple area. The atmosphere is very clams and quiet. No visitors have arrived yet because the gate will be open at 9 AM.

There are only few people around to use the toilets and showers in the early morning. They are some parents of the Samanera candidates and some of them are volunteers and care takers. They work for free and without paid. There are a number of people looking after the garden, cleaning, cooking and general management.

Figure 5.2: Early morning by the Uposatha Hall

We have wandered around and get into the kitchen, have a chat and ask them why they come here and work for free. They explain about how happy they get while working here, that is the main benefit they get. Money is not very important as much as their mind.

Figure 5.3: Early morning by the toilet building

Figure 5.4: Washing up volunteers in the Kitchen

Most volunteers are people living in the local area and not far from the temple. Their face looks very happy to do some work here. In addition, they are very friendly to stranger like us and offer us some tea, coffee and breakfast.

It is not often to get thing free with nothing in the big city like London, United Kingdom. However, in the Buddahapadipa temple Wimbledon, London, there are tea and coffee for everybody. There are many people coming to the temple to donate money for gas and electric bills, some people like to donate food and drinks. Therefore, there are many things left over more than the monks needed.

Figure 5.5: Volunteers working in the Kitchen

On the weekend, there is a stall for re-sale the donated goods such as bags of rice, coffee, tea, food cans, and toothpaste. The money received from the re- selling would save for the monk's food.

Today is the important day since it is the day for the ceremony ordination of novice monks. There will be many people attend the events, not only the parents and relatives of the Samanera candidates, but also general who believe that attend this kind of ceremony is the holy event. They will receive good luck in their life.

Figure 5.6: Volunteers cooking in the Kitchen

Figure 5.7: Practise Pali Recitation

There are a number of food and dishes have been prepared and cooks. This food is not for the monks, but also for people who come to attend the ceremony as well.

About 8 AM, it is time for morning chanting. The teacher monk, Pra Nirut, leads the Samanera candidates to join the morning changing and practise the Pali Recitation for Novice Monks' Ordination one more time.

CHAPTER 6

Things to Prepare

We have no idea about what or things we need to prepare. Furthermore, it is not easy to purchase what we need for the Novice Monks ceremony.

Figure 6.1: Things to prepare

However, on the day we visited the temple and discuss with PM Bhatsakorn. He told us we do not have to prepare anything at all, the temple have everything they need since they have the summer novice monks training course like this every year.

A few days before the ceremony, the volunteers, Pa Dong Mai, she has prepared clothes and flowers, which they are needed for all four Samanera candidates.

Figure 6.2: Flowers preparing

The four sets of flowers, candles and incenses have been arranged in the gold and silver trays. These will be used in the ordination ceremony. The flower trays are for the Samanera candidates to pay respect to the Buddha, Dhamma and Songkha. In addition, they will use them to pay their respect to their teacher monks too.

Figure 6.3: White clothes, gown and silver belt

The white shirt and white trousers have been washed, press and iron in the night before. There is a white gown with a golden rim line along the edges. The silver belt will be used for this Samanera candidates' clothes set.

This white clothes and silver belt are the special wears for only the Samanera candidate to attend the ordination of Novice monks only. Although they will use this dress for only half a day just before they change to the three pieces yellow robes later in that day, this white clothes are very important as the white symbol of purity and the gold is mean wealthy.

Thus, the Samanera candidate has to give up all of their wealth before he becomes a monk. Life as the monk does not need lots of money and wealth, just need some food to live on day by day.

Figure 6.4: Haircut equipments

In addition, there is a golden tray contain equipment consists of four scissors, fours hair shaver, four sets of candles and incense.

Figure 6.5: Razor and incense tray

The four silver bowl sets are for collecting the hair after cutting from each Samanera candidate. This equipment will be used in the Hair cutting ceremony.

The new pack of double blade razor was prepared and it must have enough for shaving four boys. Some of the Samanera candidates have their hair quite wrong. Thus, they may need more than three procedure cutting. It would start from cutting by scissor, following up by cutting with an electric shaver and finish it off with the double blade razor.

Figure 6.6: Yellow robes and monk's bag

The yellow robes and red bag for each Samanera candidate have been prepared. All clothes are packed as a set of three pieces. One set for each Samanera candidate. The monk allows to have only three pieces of clothes only. For this new novice monk, they have to learn to use clothes of what they really needs, not for luxury living life style or excessive more than they need.

Flowers always the most important things, which will be used for every ceremony in Buddist. The flowers are to pay a respect to parents and teachers. It is believed that flowers are the symbol of beauty and nice smell.

Figure 6.7: Flowers tray for Novice ceremony

A number of small coins were wrapped with silver papers and beautiful paper. This will be for Samanera candidates to give away to people who come to attend the Novice monk ceremony.

Figure 6.8: Volunteer wrap the coins for lucky money

Figure 6.9: Money lucky coins

CHAPTER 7

Offering Food

We, Buddism, have known that the monks have to held 227 rules. One of the rules is they cannot cook food for themselves. Therefore, people would offer food for the monks. Thus, they can concentrate on learning and practise Buddist Thamma.

Figure 7.1: Breakfast for venerable monks

The monks in Puddahapadipa Temple would have two meals a day. They are breakfast and Lunch. The breakfast will be between 6.15 AM to 7 AM.

However, for lunch, they have to eat before 12.00 PM. Normally, their lunch will be between 11.00-12.00.

Figure 7.2: Lunch for venerable monks

Not only the kitchen volunteer would cook food for the monks, but also other people from outsider would bring food from home. Therefore, there are many dishes and variety food styles. The monks need have eaten whatever food have been offered to them. They cannot choose or pick what they want to eat. This would make the life as the monks' simple.

Moreover, the food will be offered to the monks to eat for lunch only. They cannot keep them to eat them for the future. The strategy is they have to eat to live, just enough for only one meal at the time.

The monks have to do the reflection on food, chanting before and blessing after eating their lunch. In addition, they have to do the reflection on food before eating.

Figure 7.3: Food from people bring for the monks

The monks need to have a reflection on food before eating. This is because the food that other people offer to them are free of charge and also food is not for fun, not for pressure, not for fattening, not for beautification, only for the maintenance and nourishment of the body, and to keep it healthy.

Figure 7.4: Chanting before lunch

Figure 7.5: People attend chanting

The Samanera candidates would have their lunch at 12 PM after the monks have finished their food. At this stage, the Samanera candidates 'status is still the lay people. They have to pass the ceremony before they change the status to be Novice monks.

This would be their last lunch before they change to be the novice monks. Their behaviour will be changed and we as their mothers would not allow to touch their body anymore. It is one of the monks' rule that women are not allowed to get close or touch the monk's body.

Figure 7.6: Lunch for Samanera candidates

The remaining food after the monks finished their lunch, will be transferred to the table outside the main building by the lake. This food is for everybody, not only friends and family of the Samanera candidates, but also includes the general visitors, who just come here for visiting as tourist place in London. The beautiful Thai architecture Uposathan hall is very famous. There are many tables and chairs.

The big table is full of food and a big pot of rice, tea, coffee, milk, and water bottles are plenty for everybody. All of these are from the donation to the Buddahapadipa temple.

Figure 7.7: Lunch for everybody

CHAPTER 8

Hair Cutting Ceremony

After we finished our lunch and clean the place. All of the Samanera candidates would have their hair and eyebrow shaved.

Figure 8.1: Grandmother cuts the Samanera candidate's hair

The hair cutting ceremony starts from the Samanera candidate sit on the chairs. The head monks of the Buddahapadipa temple clip the hair of the Samanera candidates. Then, The senior of each Samanera family member start to cut their hair. We have my mother in law, who is the Samanera candidate's grandmother.

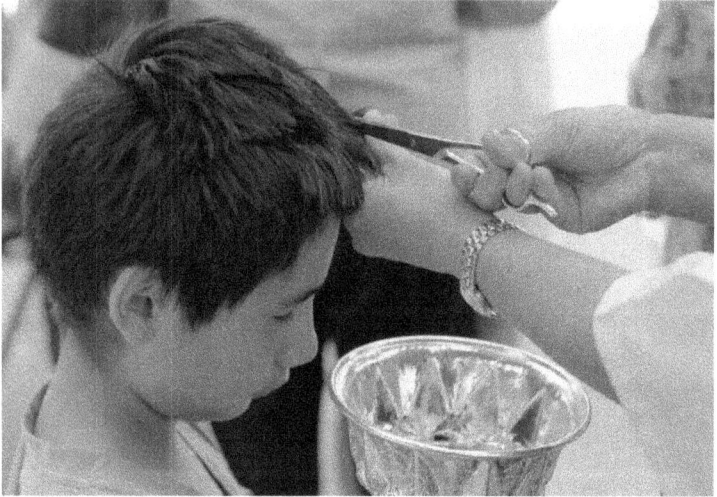

Figure 8.2: Mother cuts the Samanera candidate's hair

After that it will be the candidate's parents, family members and other people who come to attend the Ordination of Novice monks. The small bunch of his hairs would be placed in the silver bowl. This hair is a sign and symbol of respect because hair is the highest part in our body.

There are many people ask a question why the boys have to have their head and their eye brown shave in order to become the novice monk. This is because the novice monks not only not attach with their wealth, they still have to give up on their beauty and heir appearance as well. The hair on their head can change the look of the person. In addition, without their hair, less thing to worry, spend less time to wash their head and easy to look after too.

Figure 8.3: Mother holds the bowl for hair cutting

In addition, to cut the hair has another meaning of cut out from the normal people world and get into the new world of purity become a monk.

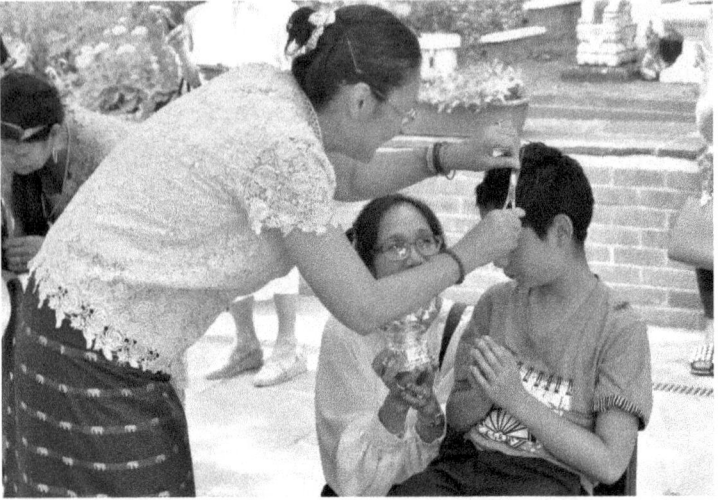

Figure 8.4: Dr. Sirilaksana Kunjara cuts the Samanera candidate's hair

Figure 8.5: Friends cut the Samanera candidate's hair

Figure 8.6: Relatives cuts the Samanera candidate's hair

Moreover, people always associate our hairs as important, it helps us look, to make us handsome and beautiful. To become a monk, they have to shave their hair on their head and eye browns. It is only convenient to clean and look after. This is one of the strategy for nothing to worry about their look or care what people will look at them, make them less worried about other people's opinion. They have to concentrate on what they are doing at present without worrying what people want them to be, what people want them to look.

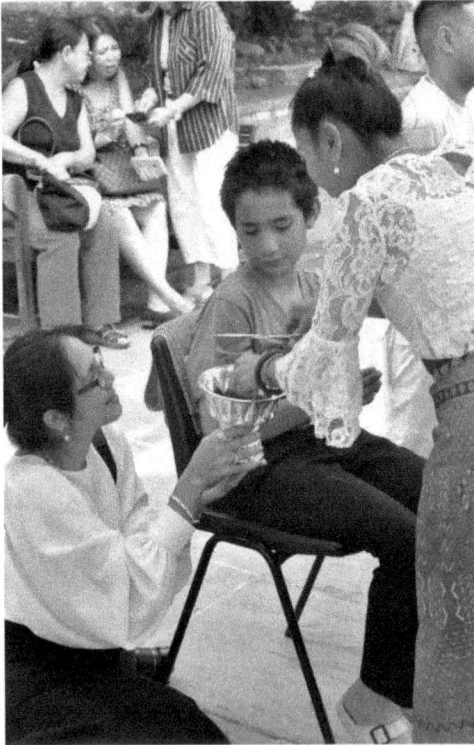

Figure 8.7: Attendee cut the Samanera candidate's hair

While people cut the Samanera candidates, they always said blessing words, wish him to be the good monk, stay on the monk's rule and wish him good luck in his life and future.

Figure 8.8: Prepare to shaves the Samanera candidate's hair

The hands of Samaner's candidate would put together like the shape of the lotus and place them between their chest. This means thank you and reply with a respect for those people, who cut his hairs. This process takes nearly an hour for everybody has a chance to cut all the four Samanera candidates. It is a blessing and happy time for all attendees.

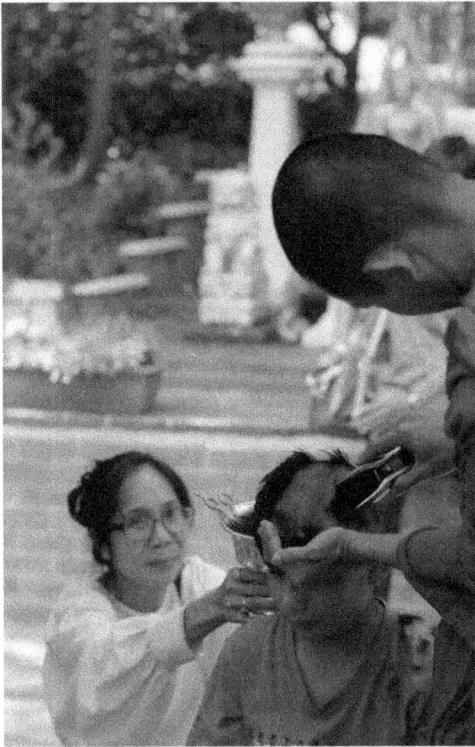

Figure 8.9: The monk shaves the Samanera candidate's hair

After all parents, family and friends have done some hair cutting. The Samanera's hair gets shorter with no style, but it does not matter since they have to be shaved off anyway.

Next the monk continues with the next process of shaving with an electric shaver by the teacher and mentor monk, Pra Nirut.

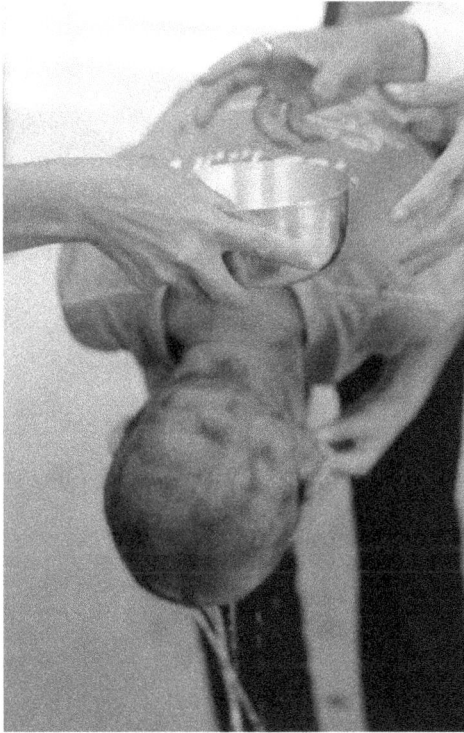

Figure 8.10: The monk pours water over the Samanera candidate's head

The water in the bucket with shampoo will be used to wash the candidate's hair and used as hair shavers gel for deep cutting. This process is unusual to see in the United Kingdom. Most of us would familiar with the shower head to wash over our head. However, a bucket full of water and a bowl to pour water over the Samanera head is a normal practise in Thailand.

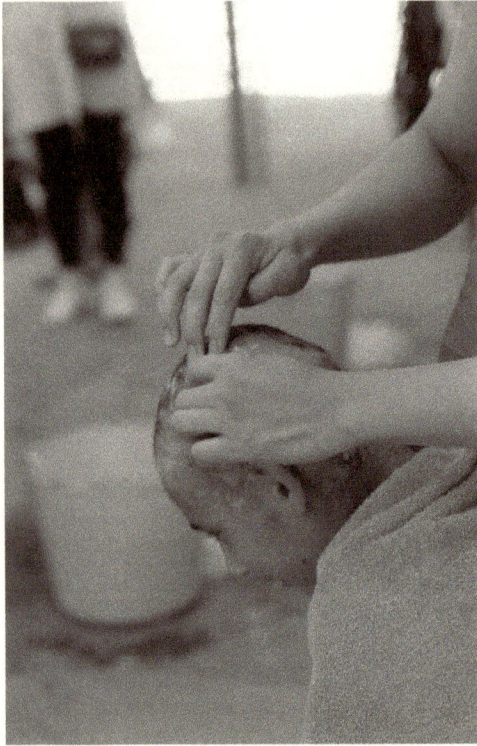

Figure 8.11: Shampoo the Samanera candidates

This hair cutting stage, the teacher monk would prepare and perform for water washing and shampoo cleaning. It seems like the teacher monks have a lot of experience in cutting for new novice monks since this temple always have a summer Samanera training course every year. They know what they are doing and it also makes the cutting hair easily as well.

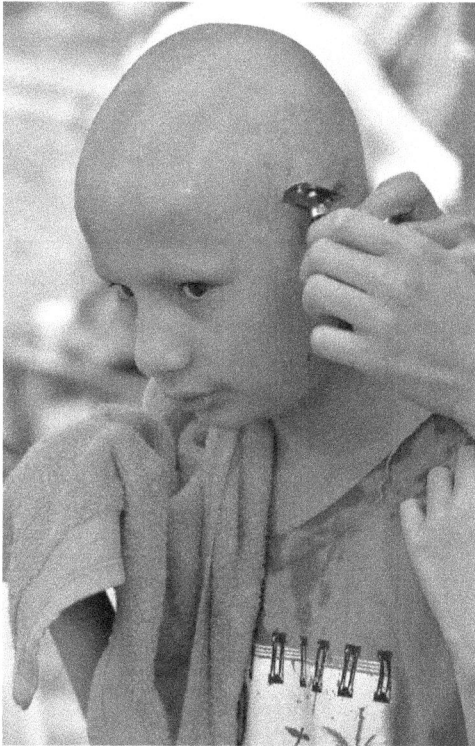

Figure 8.12: The final deep cut using razor

At the final stage of the hair cutting, the teacher monk uses a new set of doube blade razor for deep and detail hair cutting. The hair would be as short as the head skin. The teacher monk, who process this procedure is PM Aphidech. The teacher monk has to cut their own hair every two weeks. Thus, they are experts.

Figure 8.13: Final check hair cutting

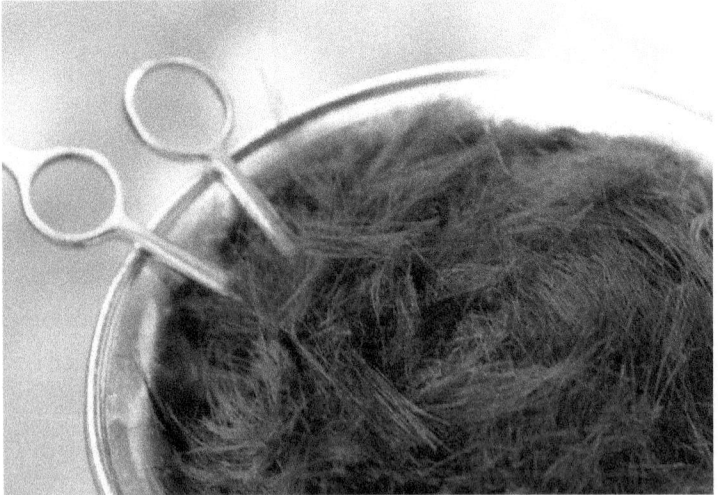

Figure 8.14: The hairs of the Samanera candidates

After the teach monk has inspected and satisfy with the Samanera candidate's hair cutting. There are some little wounds from the razor cut, but it is not serious.

Figure 8.15: The Samanera candidate's parents carry a silver bowl of hair

The teach monks would allow the Samanera candidate goes to have a quick shower and change clothes to wear white dress, which it was washed, ironing and prepared since the day before.

None of the Samenera candidate's hair has dropped on the ground, all of them put in the silver bowl, where the scissor was placed.

I was wondering what we should do with this hair. They look like the important thing. However, the teacher monks told us that we can keep a small bunch as a souvenir. The remaining hair should be placed under the big tree by the lake. It is a believe that under the tree should be moist and cool. This means the owner of those hairs will be live happy life.

CHAPTER 9

Circumambulating

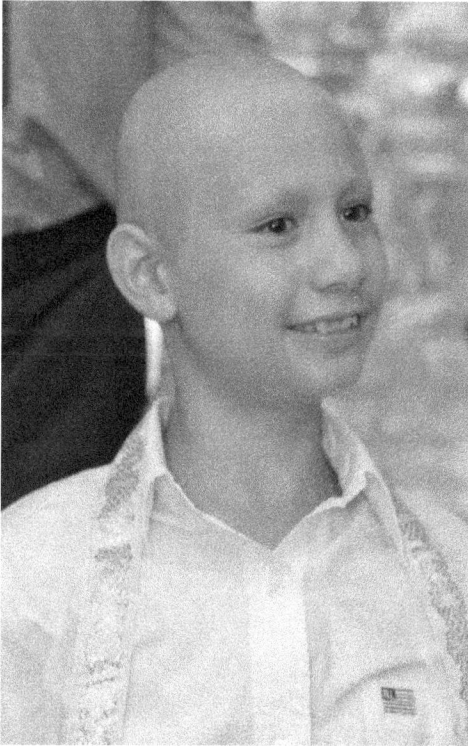

Figure 9.1: Samanera candidate uniform

After the Samanera candidates has a quick shower and get changed to white dress. This is the uniform of the Samanera candidates for ordination of novice monks. This uniform called Naka. It is a white shirt with white sarong and over with the white gown trim with gold textures around the edge.

Their head was covered with Thammaric power. There is a meaning of yellow turmeric colour, it could mean as golden. The gold always is high value substance. Another purpose is used as medicine to heal the small cut in their head skin.

Figure 9.2: Family group photo

We have a few minutes for a family photo with the Samenera candidates.

The next ceremony is the circumambulation the Uposatha all. The parade of parents, families and friends will walk along as a parade. The group of Samanera candidates will be in the front carry a set flowers with candle and incense.

Figure 9.3: Four Samanera candidate

This year 2018, there are fours Samanera candidate age between 8-12 years old. There are two Samanera candidates can speak and understand a little of Thai language, but none of them can read or write in Thai. The other two could not speak, read, write and understand Thai language at all. Therefore, this summer Samanera training course need to be conducted by the teacher monks, who can speak and understand English very well. Alternatively, there are translators come to help in teaching.

Figure 9.4: Parade set up

The parade of Samanera candidate walks around the Uposathan hall was lead by the teacher monk. Then, the roles of parent of the Samanera candidates, families, friends, and all attenders, respectively.

The direction is following the clockwise. They would walk circles around the Uposathan Hall three times. The first round is to pay respect to the Budda, the second round is to pay respect to the Dhamma and the last one is to pay respect to Songkha or the monks.

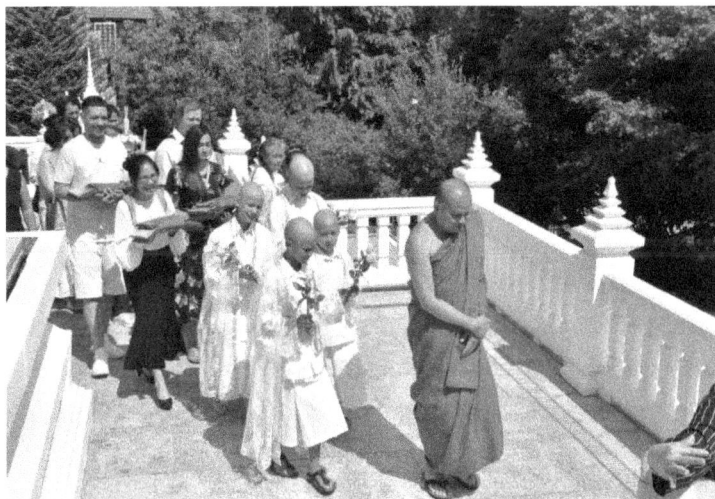

Figure 9.5: First round around the Uposathan Hall

Figure 9.6: Second round around the Uposatha hall

The parent of each Samanea candidate carries the yellow robes for their own son. This is the most joyful for every family since it was believed that their son will learn how to be a good person from the teacher monk.

In the old age many years ago, there is no school. Therefore, the only place to learn how to read, write and other knowledge is in the temple, where there are only monks are the teacher. Thus, they were called teacher monks.

Figure 9.7: The Thai music and Thai dance in the front row of the parade

With the restrict of the monks' rule, only boys have this opportunity. This is because the girl, who is opposite sex to the monk could cause, disturb or prevent the monks to practise their purity. Thus, the family who has a son in their family would count it as a fortune for them since they will get an advantage in education over the family who have only girl.

The front parade of the Samanera candidate were a band drum and entertaining, gather with a group of people dance along while they walk around the Uposathan hall. There is a meaning of this activity, this could mean a group of angels come to welcome the new monks to be.

Figure 9.8: Mrs. Taravali Jackson performs Thai dance in the parade

The ordination of novice monks event brings joy to everybody. It believes it is the best thing for the boy to become a monk and learning how to be a good boy later in their after or after they retire from the monk status.

At the end of the third round, we all reach at the star get inside the Uposatha hall.

Figure 9.9: Smiling in the parade

A group of parents, families, friends and attendees are all waiting for casting the lucky coins. This is a believe that he got this luck coin, they will lucky in earning more money in their life.

Figure 9.10: Third round around the Uposathan Hall

The Samanera candidates would walk up to the top of the stairs and turn to face their parents, families and friends just like to say good bye. After they become a monk, they will have no longer to have families and friends anymore.

They will be in another status, which not involve with normal people like us. They will become the monks, who have no greed, no jealousy, no desire in money, properties, power, wealth or fame.

The procedure of the ordination of novice monks, is quite complicated. However, there are many meanings behind each process.

Figure 9.11: The last giveaway of their properties

Figure 9.12: Joyful of receiving lucky coins

Figure 9.13: Samenera candidate casts the coins

To give up the lay person status, they will give away all of their belonging. It is the meaning of changing their status to become the monk. Therefore, all of their wealth needs to give away to anybody for the last time.

The happiness of the person who give it away and the joyfulness of the receivers, we can see clearly in their faces. The coins are not high in value.

However, it is a significant valueless for their families and friend for this important ordination of novice monk ceremony.

CHAPTER 10

Ask for Pardon

After the Samenera candidate give away all of their belonging and properties, they walk into the Uposatha hall to ask to be the monk.

Figure 10.1: Samanera candidate into the Uposathan Hall

Follow the teacher monks, they arrive at inner the Uposatha hall, where the ordination of the novice monk ceremony will conduct.

With flowers, candle and incense in their hands, they come to pay respect to the triple gem, which they are the Budda, the Thama, and the Songkha. The Buddha is the fully enlightened. The Dharma is the teachings expounded by the Buddha. The Sangha is the monastic order of Buddhism that practice the Dharma.

Figure 10.2: Pay respect to the triple gem

Normally the flower is used for the ceremony in the Buddha Temple usually would be flower lotus. This is because the shape of the lotus, look like the left and right hands put together as the symbol of respect. This action also uses in the Thai culture for greeting as well as respective to the elder, the teachers and the monk.

Figure 10.3: Flowers for parents

The Samanera candidates perform the five point prostration to their parents. The CD play the song " the value of the mother's milk", the meaning of this song is about how the mother looks after her baby from pregnancy to give birth. She still keeps looking after her baby until he grows to adulthood. Her children could not pay back for her hard working to look after them. However, what she just wants her kids to be a good person and doing well for themselves.

Next, the Samenera candidate bows to show respect to their parents and asking for forgiveness from them.

The row of parents is parallel with the role of the Samenera candidate, opposite are their mother and father. In front of them are a bowl of flowers, which will use as ask for forgiveness from their parents. They bow one for paying respect to their parents.

Figure 10.4: Flowers for parents

With their flowers in their hand, this is the symbol of respect. They will give these flowers to their parents and ask for forgiveness for whatever that they may have done something wrong or something which may be not good to their parents, make them upset with or without their intention, maybe with their physical, words or their action. They would like to say they are sorry and ask for their forgiveness.

Figure 10.5: Flower tray with candles and incense

When the parents accept the flowers from the Samenera candidates, it means they have already forgiven him for whatever he has done to make them not happy or upset. Thus, the Samenera candidate feels free of any guilt or feel any wrong doing and ready to give up the status of lay person and start the new life as a novice monk.

Figure 10.6: Ask for pardon to the parents

After that the Samanera candidate receives a set of yellow robes from their parents. The set of yellow robes consist of three pieces of clothes. The first piece is the Uttarasanga is the most prominent robe. It is sometimes also called the Kashaya robe. It is a large rectangle, about 6 by 9 feet. It can be wrapped to cover both shoulders, but most often it is wrapped to cover the left shoulder, but leaves the right shoulder and arm bare.

Figure 10.7: Parents give yellow robes to Samanera Candidate

The second piece is the Antaravasaka is worn under the Uttarasanga. It is wrapped around the waist like a sarong, covering the body from waist to knees.

The third piece is the Sanghati is an extra robe that can be wrapped around the upper body for warmth. When not in use, it is sometimes folded and draped over a shoulder. The monk is not allowed to wear anything other than this specifies.

When My Son Becomes Novice Monk in United Kingdom

CHAPTER 11

Request for going forth

After the Samenera candidate ask for forgiveness from their parents, supporters and families. Next, they pay respect to the preceptor and requesting for going forth.

Figure 11.1: Samanera candidate pays respect to preceptor

In front of the Preceptor, the Samanera candidate light the candle and incense in the receptacle. Then, they bow with five point prostrations three times. These five points consist of both of their knees, both

of their forearms and their forehead should touch
the floor at the same time.

Figure 11.2: Samanera candidate

The Samenera Candidate say words in Pali
recitation for ordination of novice monks. The
meaning of Pali in short is they would like to go for
refuge to the venerable in order to attain
Parinibbana together with the Dhamma and
Bhikkhu Sangha, may they obtain the going forth as
Samanera in the Dhamma and be accepted. They
have to ask three times. Since the Samanera
candidates cannot remember the Pali word,
therefore, the teacher monks allow them to read
from their notes.

Figure 11.3: Samanera Cadidate asks for going forth

Next, the Samanera candidate says the Pali words for yellow robes. The Pali means they beg for the going forth with their compassion to receive the yellow robes.

Again, they have to repeat the same Pali words three times. Why it has to be three times? This is because it has to be making sure that the Samanera candidate has a very intention to become the novice monks. Only if they ask once or couple times, they might change their mind afterwards.

One by one, the Samanera candidate has to come to sit in front of the head of the temple to confirm his answer and make a commitment to become a novice monk.

After the head of the temple and the group of teacher monks are satisfied with his answer and they agree on accepting him to be a part of their temple. The head of the temple will hand him a set of three pieces yellow robes.

Figure 11.4: Samanera candidate receives yellow robes

The Upajjhaya instruct them about the triple gem, the meaning and significance of ordination and use their body as preliminary objects for meditation. They are hair of the head, hair of the body, nails, teeth, and skin. The meaning is to reduce an attachment to the beauty of their body and let go of lust and desire.

Figure 11.5: Upajjhaya give the shoulder cloth

The Upajjhaya remove the first part from the set of the yellow robes, and put it over the Samanera candidate's head and arrange it to cover their left shoulder.

After they receive the remaining of the yellow robes, they move backwards on knees until they are clear of the assembled Bhikkhus. They would stand up and go to the appointed place, where there are monks help them to put their robes on.

Figure 11.6: Receive the second cloth part

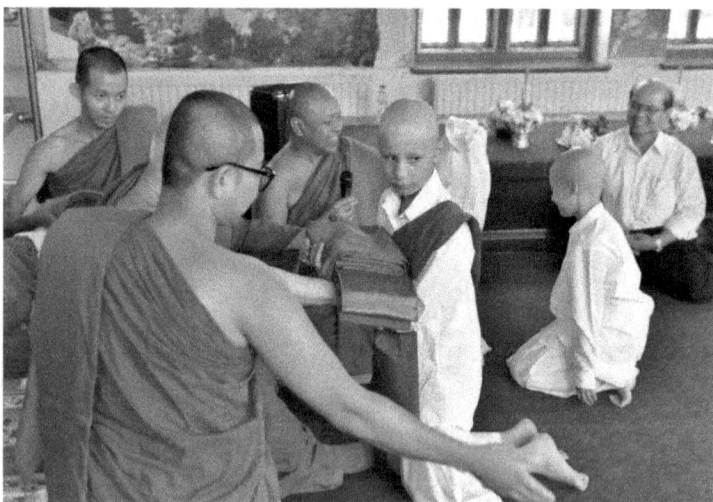

Figure 11.7: Receive all the remaining cloth

At this process the Samanera candidates have already been accepted into the Buddhapadipa temple. Therefore, they would allow to change their clothes from the white dress to the yellow robes.

The "White colour clothes" which the Samanera candidates wear after they have their head and eye brown shave, it means they are pure just like the white colour and they will be ready to absorb the good things from the Buddha , the Dhamma and the Songkha.

Figure 11.8: Help to put yellow robes on

The methodology to wear the three pieces yellow robes is complicated. This is because in the ancient way to dress up not like any of the new modern technology wearable clothes. They have to teach the method from the teacher monks to their students novice monks only. The way to learn by observing, looking, listening and practising many times a day. From the novice monk timetable, they have to get dressed between 5.30 AM to 6.00 AM, 10.00 AM to 11.00 AM and 4.30 PM to 5.30 PM.

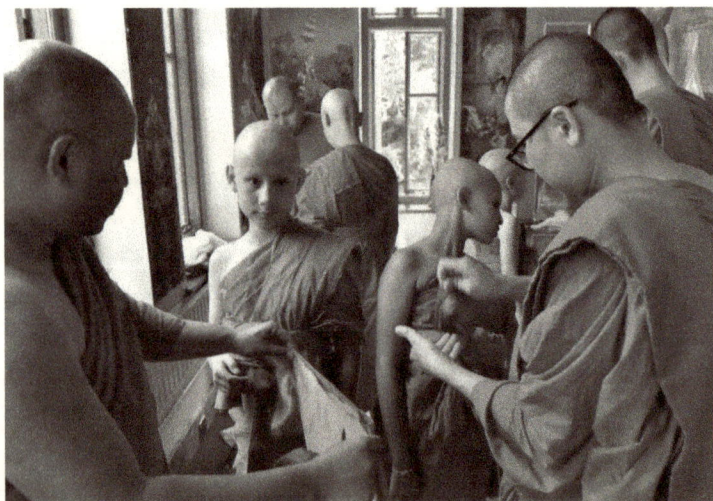

Figure 11.9: Wear yellow robes

There are four teacher monks come to help the Samanera candidate wear their yellow robes. The ratio is one teacher monks per one Samanera candidate. They have to learn how to wear the yellow robes themselves. This three piece cloth will be with them all the time. There is a methodology on how to wear them without zip or buttons, which have been the tradition more than 2,500 years ago.

Figure 11.10: First time in yellow robes

After the novice monks get changed and dress up in the yellow robes. It would not be easy for the first time for the novice monks be able to do it by themselves. They may still need help from their teacher monks to help them dress up in their yellow robes. After the final check from their teacher monks, the novice monks dress up are satisfactory, then there is a group photo with their teacher monks and the novice monks in the changing area in the Uposatha hall.

After the Samenera candidate has dress properly in their yellow robes, they return back to the main hall and sit in front of the head of the temple and a group of teacher monks.

This time they kneel down with the flower bowl in front of them. They start with the five points prostration three times before saying the Pali words to request the refuges and precepts.

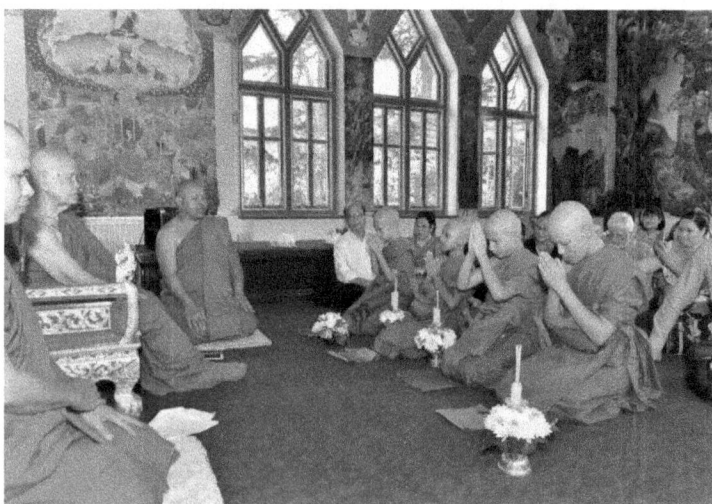

Figure 11.11: Ask for refuges and precepts

The Samenera candidate performs the five point prostrates three times with the Pali words, which means they ask for refuges and precepts. They repeat the same words three times.

Figure 11.12: Present flower bowl to the Upajjhaya

Figure 11.13: The five point prostrates

Then, the Acariya asks the Samenera candidate to concentrate on the triple gem and repeat after him sentence by sentence in Pali. The meaning includes they go to Buddha for refuge, they go to the Dhamma for refuge and they go to the Sangha for refuge. They repeat them as the first, the second and the third time.

Figure 11.14: Concentrate on the triple gem

After the Samanera candidate reply with the word "Ama Bhante" or "Yes", this is where the Acariya finishes for taking the three refuges.

At this ceremony stage, the Acariya informs the Samanera candidate that they are now the Samanera or novice monks.

Figure 11.15: Prepares flowers, candle and incense

Figure 11.16: Pay respect with flowers, candle and incense

Thus, the Samanera or novice monks, each prepares flowers, candle and incense, make them as a group. This is for to pay respect to the head monks and teach monks, who will teach them while they are in the novice monk status.

Figure 11.17: The novice monks accept the ten precepts

Now they are Novice monk, Therefore, they have to follow and study the ten precepts. They repeat ten precepts in Pali after the Acariya. They are refraining from:
(1) Killing living creatures,
(2) Taking what is not given,
(3) Unchaste conduct,
(4) Speaking falsely,

(5) Distilled and fermented intoxicants which are the occasion for carelessness,
(6) Eating at the wrong time,
(7) Dancing, singing and going to see entertainments,
(8) Wearing garlands, smartening with perfumes and beautifying with cosmetics,
(9) Lying on a high or large sleeping place,
(10) Accepting gold, silver, and money.

Figure 11.18 : Novice monks group photos

The novice monks reply that they are undertaking these ten rules of training. They repeat three times and finish with prostrates five points three times. The procedure of the ordination for novice monk is finished. Next is the teacher monks and novice monks group photos.

As a novice, he requests the senior monk to be his Preceptor and on being accepted he receives a new name in Pali. My son, his novice monk name in Pali calls "Attatdhammo" means the person who can stand all the hardship.

CHAPTER 12

Alms Round

Figure 12.1: First Alms Round

This will be the first time for the Samenera to go for Alms Round. This activity is necessary for every monks in order to survive. They will walk and people will give them some food for that day. They cannot have more than the size of their bowl, the one that they carry. They are not beggars to beg for food. However, people will give them food. Thus, they can live and study the Dhamma. They also cannot say "NO" to the food that they do like. Moreover, they neither can ask for more foods that they love, nor ask for the specific food. They just have to consume food in order to live, not to live in order to eat.

Figure 12.2: Giving a monk's bag

After they become the novice monks, they cannot work or earn money or income for a living, but they have to live from support from people.

The only their own private and important property of the novice monks can carry is as much as the size of their monk's bag. This bag made of yellow colour clothes, embroidered with the symbol and the name of the temple and size approximately 3o cm width.

Figure 12.3: Prepare for First Alms Round

The monks in Thailand would get up at 5 AM in the morning, get washed and ready for Alms Round. They will hear the bell ringing, this is the signal for all the monks in each temple to line up as the order from the highest range of seniority in the front and the youngest monks or novice monks in the end.

Normally the head of that temple will be in the front as the leader. He will walk first, following by the second older and younger monks.

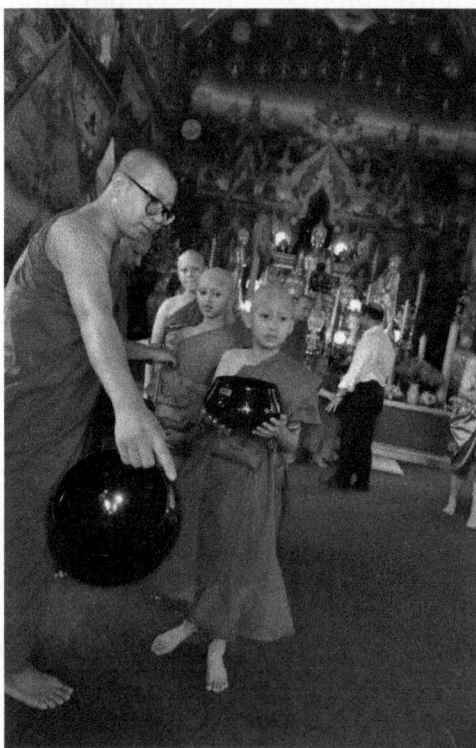

Figure 12.4: Teacher monk show where to start

The ranking in the monks system is not the same as the people aging, but the monks system would count the first year as a boy or a man become a monk and also how long he has been in the monk status.

Figure 12.5: Teacher monks explain alms round

This is a new activity for the new Samanera. Some of them have no idea at all. However, with the help and learning fro their monks, they soon get along with the monks system.

First of the all, Their teacher monks give them a small size of the black bowl, made of metal. This is their own individual bowl, which they will use for alms round and for their food container if they are the novice monks in Thailand. This is the way that the Buddha monk would live with minimum tools and equipment to survive well and healthy.

Figure 12.6: Head teacher monk shows how to walk

The head teacher monk in this group of the new Samanera is Phra Maha Pahsakorn (PM Pahsakorn) will walk out the Uposatha Hall as the leader of the new Samanera group. Phra suites (PK Sutas), he has a job to teach them how to carry the bowl for Alms round. The monk's bowl is made of metal.

Figure 12.7: Head teacher monk lead for their First Alms Round

However, some of them are made of wood or aluminium. There are many sizes, however, there are the limited how big in diameter the monks can have.

Figure 12.8: Teacher monk advises the novice monks

Normally, the size of the monk's bowl should not bigger that their own stomach. That should be big enough to contain food for one meal. That is how much they can eat for the day. This is because the monk cannot keep food for the future.

The food they get from the Alms round is just enough to eat for that day. If they are some food left

over after they finish eating. They have to give that
food away or bin them.

Figure 12.9: People put their food in the novice monk's
bowl

The novice monks walk followed each other in the
role. They have to walk not too fast and not too
slow. Their walking pace is fast enough for the row
to move forward, and slow enough for people have
time to put food in their bowl. They are not allowed

to stand and waiting for people to put things in their bowl because the novice monks are not the beggars.

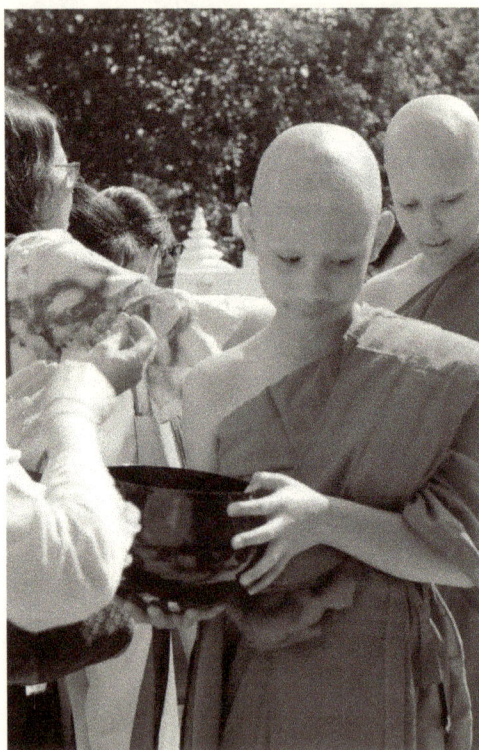

Figure 12.10: Novice monks go Alms Round

The sequence and step of walking for Alms round are guided by the teacher monk, Phra Nirut (P Nirut). He is the closest point of this group of new Samanera. The Samanera would inform and discuss with him about any concern and problems,

When My Son Becomes Novice Monk in United Kingdom

including any need. In addition, he is the youngest monks in this temple and understand English very well.

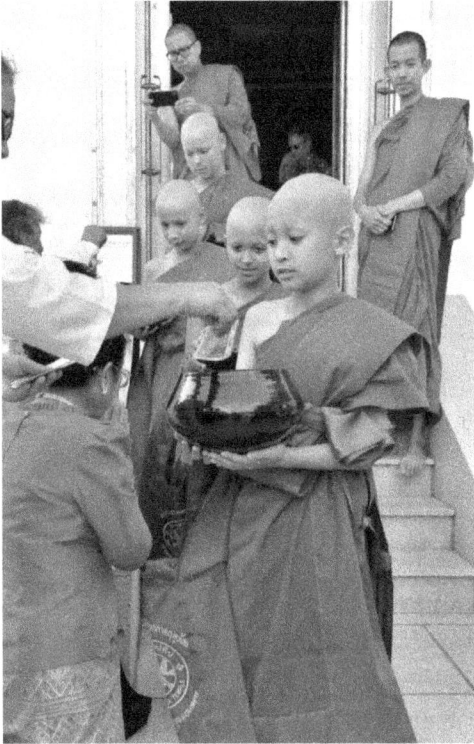

Figure 12.11: Row of novice monks Alms Round

The most important procedure of Alms round is quiet and concentrate. The Samanera cannot or allow to chat or talk to people who give them food in his bowl. They cannot request or ask their parents, family and friends give or do things for them. They cannot request any favour. This is because they are not normal people anymore, but they are in the status of the monks, who has no friends or family and their main job is to study the Dhamma.

Figure 12.12: Alms Round under supervised

The Novice monks or Samanera will walk as a row follow each other carry a bowl. They are not allowed to chase each other up or racing to be in the front of the queue.

This group of new novice monks seem to know and understand what they have to do although it is their first time for some of them. The most happiness people is their parents, family and friends.

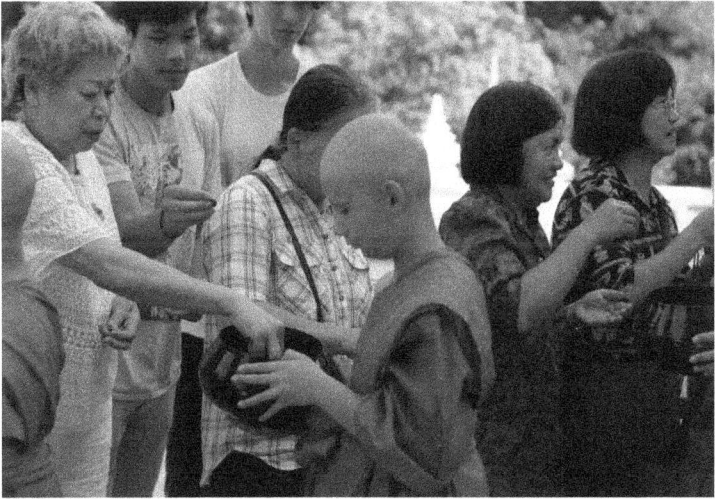

Figure 12.13: Novice monks and his bowl

Figure 12.14: Row of people waiting for alms round

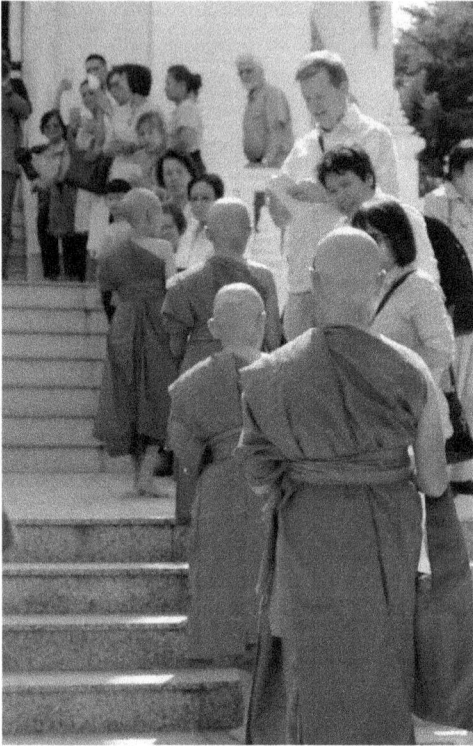

Figure 12.15: Go back after an alms round

They will not allow to look inside their bowl or curious about what people give them. They can just accept whatever in their bowl.

In Buddhism, the alms is the respect given by a lay Buddhist to a Buddhist monk. People always put the best food that they have to the monk bowl. They show their respect to the monks. This is because the monks in the person, who carry on the Dhamma of the Budda and transfer this knowledge to general people.

Figure 12.16: Finish from the alms round

A bowl and one small bag are the only two things that necessary for the monk to live on. This bag is to carry his own belonging such as medicine, small documents and private necessary things.

Figure 12.17: The group photo with their monk bag

This group of children age 8 -12 years old, comes from different town in the United Kingdom. Today they make a commitment to become the novice monks at the Buddhapadipa temple and they will practise the perceive ten, learn the Buddha story, practise meditation and study the Dhamma.

CHAPTER 13

Novice Monk Schedule

Become a Novice monk or Samanera in United Kingdom is not the same as become a Samanera in Thailand. It is not only the weather is different, but also the culture and environment are not the same.

Figure 13.1: Novice monks practise

Most of the time the weather in Thailand is hot. Although we say that there are three seasons in Thailand. However, it still said that the raining season and winter season, the weather is still hot.

The average temperature is rarely lower than 30 degree C. Therefore, the yellow robes that the monks wear is enough.

Figure 13.2: New group of Novice monks

However, with the weather in the United Kingdom, there are four seasons. However, there are only a couple days that the temperature higher than 20 degree C. In winter the temperature could drop under zero degree, thus the three pieces yellow robes may be not enough to keep the human body warm. Therefore, the additional clothes such as hat, gloves, inner layer and overcoat may be needed.

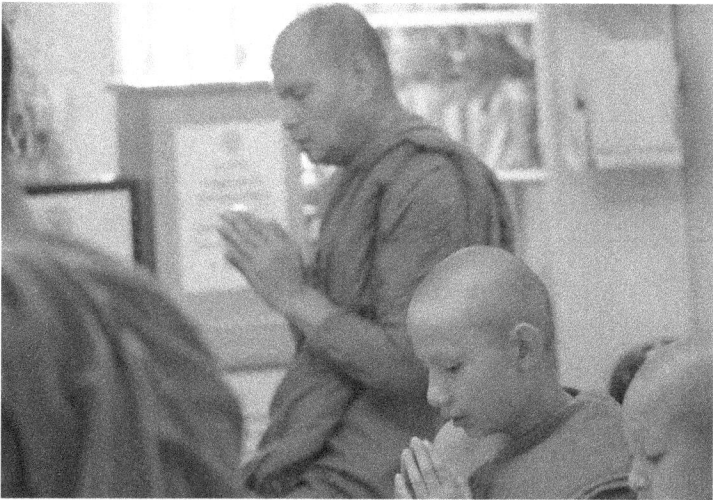

Figure 13.3: Novice monks learn chanting

Being the Samanera has to practise ten perceives as said earlier. In addition, the Samanera has to follow the daily schedule as time table as shown below.

5.30 -6.00 AM   Get up and get dressed
6.15-7.00 AM   Breakfast
8.00-8.30 AM   Morning chanting
8.30-9.00 AM   Dhamma for novice monks
9.00-10.00 AM   Cleaning
10.00-11.00 AM   Practise manner
11.00-12.00 PM   Lunch
12.00-1.30 PM   Rest and private time
1.30-3.30 PM   Learning about Buddha
3.30-4.30 PM   Beverage

4.30-5.30 PM	Wash and private activity
6.00-6.30 PM	Evening chanting
6.30-7.30 PM	Vipassana meditation
7.30-8.00 PM	Beverage
8.00-9.30 PM	Vipassana meditation
9.30 PM	Light out and sleep

Figure 13.4: Morning chanting at 8.00-8.30 AM

This daily schedule is mixing between activities in learning and meditation. However, this would help the new Samanera get on and make themselves familiar with their routine.

The most challenge for the novice monks, is they have to get up very early at 5.30 AM. Normally, children in the United Kingdom around the age 8-12 year old, they will get up about 7 AM and bed time about 8 PM. They tend to have a 12 hour sleep per day.

However, the children in Thailand tend to sleep less than the children in the United Kingdom. They sleep average about 8 hours per day. This may be because of the weather and the period of the sunlight.

Figure 13.5: Morning chants with teacher monks

Another new routine of the novice monks, is the chanting in the morning and evening. At the end of the chanting, they have to do the radiation of loving and kindness to themselves and to all beings. This includes transference of merit to their family, friends, teachers, gods, supports, ghosts, enemies, and all beings. This benefit not only to themselves, but also for other people as well.

The most interesting thing about this chanting is they have to recite the five remembrances, which are nature to grow old, have ill health, die, separated and consequences of their actions. These are the true nature.

Figure 13.6: Evening chanting at 6.00-7.00 PM

The new Samanera will chanting in Pali language as indicated in the Pali book with written in English. The pronunciation will be in English but the sound of the word is Pali language. All of the Samanera can read English, however, the Pali chanting is not easy to remember. Therefore, they have to sound the Pali word follow the teacher monks.

Figure 13.7: people join the chanting

The teacher monks will lead the new Samanera group in the morning chanting and practise Vipassana meditation every morning. Although the morning chanting session will last only 30 minutes, however, with about 5 minutes would be quite a long time for the new Samanera who never sit still, close their eyes and be quiet.

There are some people coming to join during the morning and evening chanting and follow with the short meditation. All people are welcome. Some people come from far away, from the another town far from London.

Figure 13.8: Group photo after morning chanting

However, most people who are volunteering to help do some jobs in the temple are live locally. There are a number international with various nationalities who are interested in meditation, will come to learn and practise meditation in this Buddhapadipa temple, which the temple open an 1-2 hours evening meditation course on the weekday and whole day on the weekend. Moreover, there are a long courses such as three days or ten day course in some months of the year and running from time to time.

CHAPTER 14

Practise Meditation

Figure 14.1: Learn how to sit

There is a working team of the teacher monks, who will respond for each activity following the time table and novice monks schedule of every day. The teacher monks are Phra Thepbhavanamongkol, PM Bhatsakorn, PM Apidech, PM Kitiwat, PK Sutus, PK Lom, Worapon, and P Nirut.

Phra Thepbhavanamongkol is the head of the monks in the Buddhapadipa Temple Wimbledon.

He is the oldest monks, not only the physical age, but ago the ages since he became the monk. He has a deep knowledge in Buddhism since he used to live and practise meditation in Srilan ka for many years. In addition, he can speak and understand many languages such as English, Pali, Thai, some of the South Asia and South East languages .

Figure 14.2: The advice from the head of the temple

Most of this new Samanera or novice monks were born and live in the United Kingdom. Their everyday life and activity is like normal British children. Thus, it is not easy for them to sit and perform five point prostration easily.

First of all, they have to learn and familiar themselves how to sit on the floor both cross legs and sit on their heels.

Figure 14.3: Novice monks sit on their heels

It is not quite easy for some of the novice monks to sit on their heels, and control their torso upper body to make it straight and hold the body to sit upright. However, the novice monks physical body is still no full growth as the man. Thus, they have some flexibility to able sit on the floor with their cross legs. Although they have their body build structure as the British children, but their body can be more flexible if they have been practising since they were young.

Figure 14.4: Novice monks learn five point prostration

The meditation class has been taught by the teacher monk, P Worapon. He has many years teaching experience and conducts a number of meditation courses for general people, nuns, and monks in Thailand and aboard.

Not only the novice monks have been taught how to sit on the floor, they also have to learn how to get up from sitting position as well. This is because their clothes. The three piece of yellow robes that they wear were not sewn together. Therefore, they have to be extremely careful when they get up, otherwise they would become naked in the public.

Figure 14.5: Novice monks practise sitting meditation

Figure 14.6: Sitting meditation under the tree

The best practise of the meditation is sitting cross legs. The triangle on the leg base with the body sit straight uphold, the weight of the body would balance. Therefore, this is the most comfortable position for the novice monks be able to sit and concentrate on their own breathing longer than other sitting position.

Figure 14.7: Novice monks practise walking meditation

The meditation can be practised in many forms. The teach monk explains to the novice monks that there are methods to learn the meditation can be practised in many forms. This includes sitting, standing, working, and sleeping.

Figure 14.8: Novice monks practise standing meditation

This summer novice monk training course, the novice monks will learn and practise three types of meditation. They are cross legs sitting meditation, standing meditation and walking meditation.

This class was conducted in the evening between 8.20 PM to 9.15 PM. There is a boy in white clothes came to learn the meditation technique with the novice monks. As it mentions before, there are meditation course teach in this temple and people who are interested in learning and like to practise are always welcome.

Figure 14.9 Novice monks walking and meditation

While the novice monk practise walking and standing, both of their hands should put together in front of their body. Their concentration will be at their foot while they walk. Every step that they lift their leg, they must know and acknowledge where their foot will place. Further, when the foot touches the surface, they will feel the touch and acknowledge it. When their heel starts to leave the floor in order to move forward, they will keep looking at their own action and realise that one of their feet is in the air before that foot reaches the ground level.

Figure 14.10: Novice monks ask questions

As we expected, at the end of the meditation class, there are a lot of questions come from the novice monks. This is because this is their first time to learn how to practise the meditation.

In addition, the age of this novice monk group is still children between 8 years old to 12 years old, they like to learn new thing and explore many options. The nature of the kids in this age, they like to move around and be active. Thus, it is quite difficult for them to stay still and keep quiet for such a long time during the meditation course.

CHAPTER 15

Wearing Robes

Figure 15.1: Learning to wear the yellow robes

The monk uniform is the three pieces yellow robes. We always see the monks wear them beautifully. However, we have never known that there is a certain method to wear the yellow robes without the leather belt like the modern day.

The yellow robes were used more than two thousand five hundred years ago. The leather belts may be not available at that time. Therefore, the monks have to use the materials which available in the local area and adapt to use with their yellow robes.

Figure 15.2: One to one teach how to wear the yellow robes

The yellow robes is not as simple as the modern clothes, which we use zip and button to fasten the clothes together to fix along our body shape. The good thing about the robes is they are standard size and it can fit all size and shape of the monks.

The way that the teacher monks teach the novice monks how to wear their three pieces yellow robes is they use the method one to one. This is a pretty complicated method of rolling, twisting and crossing over each piece. Therefore, one teacher monk will conduct and show each novice monk.

Figure 15.3: Practise wearing the yellow robes

After that, the teacher monk will let each of their novice monk students try to wear their own yellow robes by themselves.

As it is shown in these pictures, the novice monk's yellow robes, which were worn by themselves are not as neat and beautiful as their teacher monks, whose have many years practise in wearing the yellow robes. Furthermore, the yellow robes are pretty big for their small hands to hold both ends at the same time.

Figure 15.4: Wear the yellow robes by themselves

With the standard size of the yellow robes, some pieces may quite big and wide for a novice monk can handle. However, their teacher monks show them how to manage the big piece of the yellow robes. This piece is used to cover the remaining of the body after the first and the second piece.

The first piece which used to cover one of the shoulders on the left hand side and on the top part of the body. The second piece of the yellow robes is used to cover the below part of the body. This would wear it like sarong and use a string tied around their waist to secure the bottom part.

Figure 15.5: Fold the yellow robes

Figure 15.6: Final checking the yellow robes

The biggest piece would be folded backward and forward along the widest length. For a little small monk, this would fold smaller to fit his height.

It is amazing to see how the monks wear their clothes without modern technology and new materials. Furthermore, the methodology of wearing the robes is carried on by teaching one by one. From previous generation to generation.

CHAPTER 16

Novice monk Tasks

Figure 16.1: Cleaning the temple area

Every morning between 9 AM and 10 AM, the novice monks have a duty to clean the temple area.

During summer month in the United Kingdom, the weather is warm and a lot of the sunlight. It is a good activity for this novice monk to get some exercise after their breakfast.

Each morning the teacher monk, P Nirut, will give them an assignment which area they have to clean. Most of their jobs would sweep the floor, clear the leaves and tidy the surround thing.

One morning, the novice monk was assigned the job to clear the leaves and the floor by the back gate entrance to the kitchen area. This gate is used for transfer the goods and heavy truck into the kitchen.

Figure 16.2: Back gate entrance cleaning

The cleaning and clearing the leaves are every day job. The novice monks start working from the side building by the kitchen gate first before moving over to the other area around the temple.

Some of the novice monks have never done any cleaning jobs in their own home before. Their parents may think that they are too young for the household job. However, the cleaning task creates more fun time for the novice monks as well as learning how to use the cleaning tools. Also, this is a kind of exercise and prevent the laziness for them after they have their breakfast.

Figure 16.3: Leaves clearing by the fence

The job proposes for the clearing the leaves task for the novice monk is not only make the temple area clean, but also the novice monk themselves start to notice some little animals such as ants, worms, and other bugs which live on the plants and leaves.

Figure 16.4: Dusting in front of the main building

They would learn and realise that those animals, although they are smaller than human like the novice monk themselves, they also love their own life. This nature would teach the Dhamma to the novice monk about the life cycle from birth until death.

In addition, they will see some baby bugs, the old bugs and the dead bugs. These animals are just like us, one day we all will be death like them too. Therefore, the novice monk should have loving and kindness.

Figure 16.5: Road clearing of the visitor car park

Furthermore, they would understand deeply the words that they have been recited every day about the five remembrances about the nature to grow old, the nature to have ill health, the nature to die, the nature to change.

This includes everyone that they love, there is no way to escape being separated from them. Also, they cannot escape the consequences of their own actions. While their hands are doing the cleaning job, their minds are concentrated. This is a kind of working meditation.

Figure 16.6: Entrance cleaning every day task

Figure 16.7: Clearing under the trees

Another morning, the novice monk was assigned to clean the entrance areas along the road and the footpath. This is the main entrance for visitors' cars to drive through to the car park next to the toilet building. This road will be busy just before lunch time since people like to come to the temple and provide food to the monks.

In the morning is quiet time in the temple area. Therefore, it is pretty safe for the novice monk would work in cleaning and clearing the leaves

While the novice monk sweep the floor in front of the main building, they found some dust and small bit of pieces. If it was before, they may not notice it at all.

However, when they become the novice monk, they start to see the small things in the bin and notice little animals. This helps them to see what was thrown away because people do not want it. The cleaning task was given to them, not only the teacher monks want the temple area will be clean, it is also the clever way to teach the novice monks to see and observe the real life.

Figure 16.8: Cleaning in front the main building

Figure 16.9: Novice monk observes the objects

One of the main tasks for the novice monk is feeding the animals, which live inside the Buddhapadipa Temple boundary. The original geography, there is a pound belong to the temple. Also, a small forest where there are many kinds of birds, ducks and other animals.

Figure 16.10: Birds and ducks

Every morning after the novice monk has their breakfast and some of the food remaining, they would give to some animals which live around there. Their favourite animal is the duck family, which live permanently by the bank of the pond.

It is interesting to see the four of the novice monks always do the activity together. This may be because they are in the similar age. Also, they grow up in the same environment in the United Kingdom. Furthermore, they are the only child in their family.

Figure 16.11: Breads for the fishes

Figure 16.12: Pound behind the main building

Without brothers, sisters and any sibling, the only child in a family always counts as being independent and be selfish. However, when these four children spent time together in the summer novice monks training camp, they get along very well. Some how they just act like brothers come from the same family.

In addition, they share things between themselves and give advice to each others. In the first few days, since the temple is a strange place and the teach monks are strangers to them, one of the novice monks feel home sick, the group of this novice monk comforts each other very well.

Figure 16.13: Novice monk feeds the ducks

This is their duty to feed the animals and the ducks in the pond every morning. It is the task that they enjoy very much. They grow very fond of the duck family. Not only that, the ducks themselves feel familiar with the group of novice monk too. Anytime when they saw a group of the boys wearing yellow robes, the ducks and the birds would gather together and come to close to the novice monk.

The animals must feel safe and they know that they will get their food from this group and there is no danger to their life either.

Figure 16.14: Novice monk observe the water animals

While their children become a novice monk at the Buddhapadipa Temple, their parents become volunteer to help cut the grass and repair the toilets and showers.

Figure 16.15: Novice monk's parents repairing the showers and toilets

This is a normal way for the British parents since this is their son first time to join the Summer novice monks training course at the Buddhapadipa

Temple. They would like to make sure that their kids are fine with the pace and the monk's system.

Figure 16.16: Novice monk's parents change new showers in the toilet building

Some of the parents would stay over for a few days until they feel confident and happy that their son could adapt to the place and people, especially the group of the new novice monks. Moreover, these parents provide their support and services free of charge as the temple 's volunteer while they stay in the temple to observe and support their children.

When My Son Becomes Novice Monk in United Kingdom

CHAPTER 17

Mural Painting

Figure 17.1: Teacher monk shows the mural painting

This afternoon the teach monk, PM Bhatsakorn, leads the novice monk group to the Uposatha Hall. There are mural paintings around the walls and ceiling about the Buddha history.

Some pictures are small and some are big, some make sense and easy to understand the story without words or any letters to explain the meaning of the painting. However, some pictures are weir and should not be there.

Figure 17.2: Study painting in the Uposatha hall

PM Bhatsakorn, the teacher monk starts to show them the painting on the top left hand side. The picture of the woman gives birth to a boy under the big tree. There are lotus flowers under the boy's foot when he walks.

The teacher monk uses the laser pointer to show them and explain the meaning of lotus flowers, the big tree and a group of people around the boy. That is the painting tell the story about when the Buddha was born. He was a son of the Indian King. His mother gives birth to him while she travels to visit her parents at another city. It was a culture at that time that when the woman pregnant,she has to go to her parent's house to give birth. Normally, they will start to make a journey quite early before the due date. However, for this case the baby was arrived early while they are on their way. Thus, she has to give birth in the forest under the tree.

To make it as the wonderful story about the birth of the Buddha, therefore, he can walk immediately and his foot dot not get dirty from walking. Thus, the lotus flowers were created there.

Figure 17.3: The birth of the Buddha

However, the novice monks have many questions to ask the teacher monk such as why the mother gives birth while standing? Why the baby grows up so quickly just like the boy size and also can the baby grow instantly and walk immediately?

Figure 17.4: Life of the Buddha in painting

However, the story is the story. The teacher monk can explain some questions and cannot explain in scientific fact. The novice monk starts to learn the story of the Buddha from 1.30 PM until 3.30 PM.

Figure 17.5: Storytelling in paintings

Figure 17.6: The teacher monk explains the meaning

They enjoyed listening to the story and look at the painting at the time. The next picture is the Buddha sleep and dream. The novice monks ask their teacher monk why the size of the Buddha is bigger than other people including the angels.

Figure 17.7: Enchantment painting

The painting is very colourful and beautiful too. What the novice monks like most is the story behind each painting. However, there is no rectangular line to separate each picture. These pictures come in different shapes and size. The theme also different as the story be told, including the colour tone which use in each panel.

There are many hidden pictures such as the coke can, the aeroplane and the Thai Airways, in the painting, which they are in the modern day. However, they are appeared mix in the painting told us the story of more than two thousand five hundred years ago.

Figure 17.8: Giant's eye

We have met one of the painters, Mr. Kitisak Nuallak. He came to paint the pictures in the Uposathan hall about 30 years ago. He told us that there was a group of painters and artists about 60 people from Thailand, who are expert in Buddha painting and temple painting. This is because the painting technique is different between paint on the wall and paint on the paper or canvas.

Figure 17.9: The painter, Mr. Kitisak Nuallak

Mr. Kitisak, the painter and artist is the only one still live in the United Kingdom after the painting job inside the Uposathan Hall had finished.

His job as the painter in the Buddhapadipa temple is not only the paint inside the Uposatha hall only, but also include the decorating in other buildings, which present the Thai culture, tradition and arts such as the Bell Tower. And some repairing pictures inside the Uposatha hall when they got damaged.

Figure 17.10: Flighting and wars

The pictures of the two elephants and their army flighting above the picture of a big giant angry eye are represented about the war in the human world. The Buddha was floating above in the triangle with enlightened around him. The painting on this wall could tell us about the Buddha stay above the flight and over anything.

These mural paintings do not have the description for each picture like the painting shown in the museum. The temple paintings usually, the painters and the artists will draw and paints the story about the Buddha's life, which he was born in many times before he becomes the Buddha.

Figure 17.11: Buddha enlightenment

Figure 17.12: Buddha teaches the Dhamma

The paintings show the pictures of the Buddha travel to many places and teaches the Dhamma to the people. The first five people that he visited were his old teachers.

During he lives his life as the monk, he has a lot of followers and people respect his Dhamma. This is because his Dhamma is truth, useful and create benefit to the people.

Figure 17.13: Heaven and hell painting

The painting about the heaven and hell is the most interesting pictures for the novice monk. The teacher monk explains to them a simple way. If they want to go to the heaven, they have to be a good boy and do the good thing.

Figure 17.14: Discussion about the heaven

Some paintings are too much in details and it is so untruth and unbelievable. They are so contrasted with the real life. However, there are some true behind those pictures.

However, if they do thing bad, they will go to hell instead. As the painting shows the heaven is high above the floor where the people live and the hell just below the underground. Thus, the novice monk understands that in order to go up to the heaven, they must be able to fly. Opposite to the heaven, go down to hell they have to dig a hole into the ground.

Figure 17.15: Disagree about the meaning

The painting heaven and hell create a lot of questions among the novice monks. This is because they have been born in the United Kingdom and have never believed in anything easily.

The story about heaven and hell is further far that their everyday life. Thus, it is easy for the teacher try to answer many questions from the novice monks.

This is the interesting point about the mural paintings in the Uposatha hall. Although people look and see at the same pictures, but they understand the meanings of each pictures are different. In addition, it does not matter when we look at the same pictures, the meaning would change each time. This is the Dhamma behind those mural paintings.

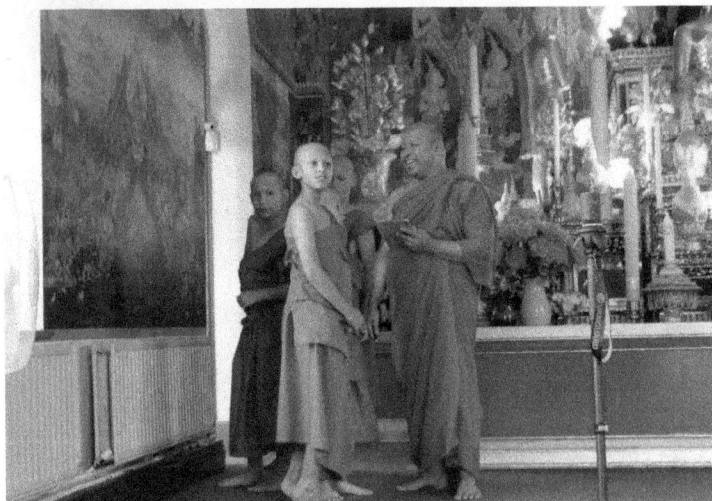

Figure 17.16: Answer the questions

There are many questions from the novice monks that the teacher monk cannot answer. This is not because he does not know the answers, but he does not know how to explain and make the children age 8 -12 years old understand easily.

Moreover, these children were not born and live in Thailand, which the kids there would have a believe from their family inject to their mind since they were a baby and grow up with the believe in Buddhism.

Figure 17.17: Thai arts ceiling decoration

Figure 17.18: Number of the Buddha

The painting and decorating in the ceiling provide information about the Buddha story and the decoration like the flower lotus shape. This is because the flower lotus is the symbol of respect to the Buddha and his Dhamma.

Figure 17.19: Listening to the story

There are many topics that the novice monks and their teacher monk discuss together. They either do not believe anything easily nor accept the Buddha story completely. However, there are some points that they have all agreed together such as they will be a good person and they will not kill any animals or people. That was the conclusion of the mural painting study.

Finally, the teacher monk and his student, the novice monks pay their respect with five point prostration three times. These are for the Buddha, the Dhamma and the Songkha.

Figure 17.20: Pay respect to the Buddha

When My Son Becomes Novice Monk in United Kingdom

CHAPTER 18

Novice Hut

Figure 18.1: The novice hut

On the first night when the Samanera candidates arrive at the temple, the teacher monks allow them to stay in the main building. However, when they become the novice monks and they are familiar with the temple, they have their own place. They give it a name "The novice hut"

The novice hut is the place where the group of the new novice monks sleeps. This building is used as the Sunday school for kids to learn Thai language, tradition and culture, such as Thai dancing, Thai music and Thai instruments.

Figure 18.2: The teacher monk visit the novice hut

During the daytime, some of the teacher monks will come to talk and ask how the novice monks are. They feel free to tell them anything that they want, what they worried and discuss the problem solution. An the nigh time, their teacher and mentor monk, P Nirut, will come and check their safety and tell them it is their bedtime. The group of this novice monk will go to clean their teeth and do privately in the toilet building and back to their novice hut. The light would turn off at 9.30 PM.

This building is not far from the toilet building. Therefore, it is convenient for them when they need to use the toilet in the night.

Figure 18.3: Playing in front of the novice hut

Moreover, as the novice monks still quite young at their age, sometime they quite noisy playing during their free time. Thus, it is better for the teacher monks to separate their novice sleeping place from the main building.

The novice monks have prepared their own sleeping bag, bed sheet, duvet and pillows. The novice monk rule of practise about sleeping is they should not sleep on the thick comfortable bed. This will make them reluctant to get up in the morning.

Therefore, their bed is simple with a thin bed sheet lay on the floor.

All four of the novice monks sleep together in the same room. The room is not very big, but not too small. All of them can manage to secure each corner as their bed station. They do not have many things belonging to them. Also, the only clothes they need is the three pieces yellow robes, which they wear on their own body.

The novice monks will live in a simple way, they just need somewhere to sleep, with a blanket and sheet to cover their body in the night. However, there are few duvets available if they need some.

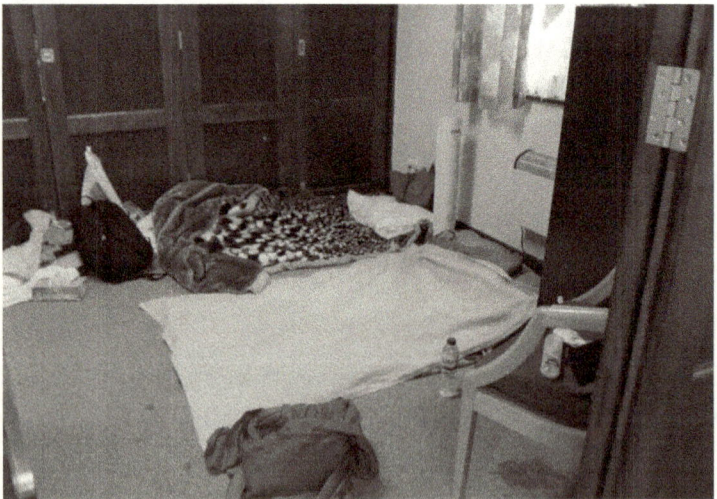

Figure 18.4: The novice monk's bed

Figure 18.5: Free time in the novice hut

During their break, the novice monks like to play games together. They will go and stay in the group of four. They were called themselves "The Fantastic Four". Their behaviour is just like normal kids. They like to play games, like to draw pictures, run around the garden and like to fold the paper aeroplane.

In the morning and in the evening, the teacher monk who is their mentor, P Nirut, will go to call them and lead them to the main building for morning and evening chanting. The novice monks would walk along the line and follow the teacher monk.

Figure 18.6: Go to the morning chanting

Figure 18.7: Walk to the evening chanting

CHAPTER 19

Breakfast for Novice Monks

The Novice monks need to have their breakfast very early at 6.16 AM to 7.00AM. This is because they have no dinner in the evening. Although they have a beverage, but only the liquid drink, may not be enough to stand their hungry.

Figure 19.1: Novice monks have breakfast

Figure 19.2: Breakfast cooking in the Kitchen

Figure 19.3: Breakfast for teacher monks

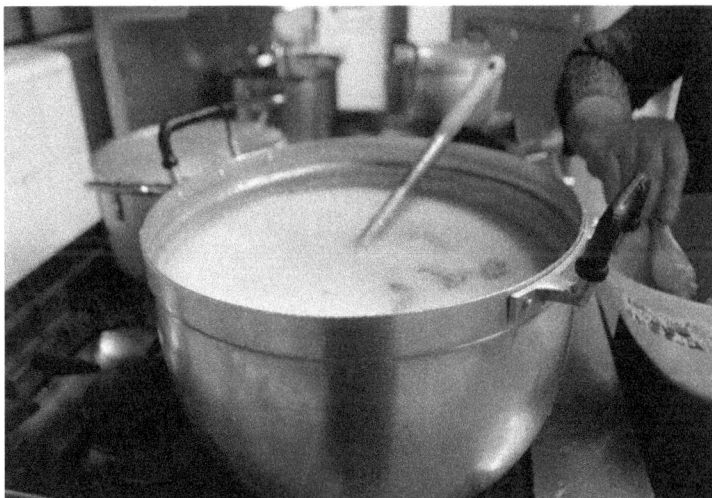

Figure 19.4: Breakfast for monks, nuns and volunteers

Figure 19.5: Thai Breakfast for teacher monks

Figure 19.6: Chinese Breakfast

Moreover, they are in the age of growing in their physical body. In order to have their breakfast before 7 AM, thus, they have to get up at 5.30 AM. They have to get washed, dressed and walk from their sleeping hut to the main building for their food.

Since the breakfast time is very early, therefore, the volunteer chef has to cook breakfast for the monks, teacher monks and novice monks in the kitchen.

Most of the teacher monks are Thai and come from Thailand. Therefore, the chef always cooks Thai breakfast or Chinese meals. These foods are not only for the monks, but also for the volunteer, who come to help the temple in cleaning and repairing.

Figure 19.7: Breakfast set up for novice monks

The breakfast for the novice monks are different from the teacher monks. This is because most of the novice monks were born in the United Kingdom, they are familiar with British food more than their Thai teacher monks. Their breakfast would be cereals, eggs, bacon, toast, and sausages. They would have hot drink such as chocolate drinks, milk with their breakfast and fruit juices.

The Volunteer care taker, Mr. Kitisak, would set the table for the teacher monks and the novice monks before they arrive at 6.15 AM. He will set the table with four sets of fork and knife for the novice monks, while fork and spoon for the teacher monks.

Most of the teacher monks have been living in the United Kingdom for many years. They get used to the cold weather and familiar themselves with the hot drink such as tea and coffee. Thus, one of the main jobs of the volunteer care taker is preparing the hot water in a 20 litter kettle tank.

Not every teacher monk come to have breakfast in the morning. Some of them would practise meditation and prefer to have only one meal a day, which is the lunch time, which is the main meal of the day.

Figure 19.8: Breakfast set up for the teacher monks

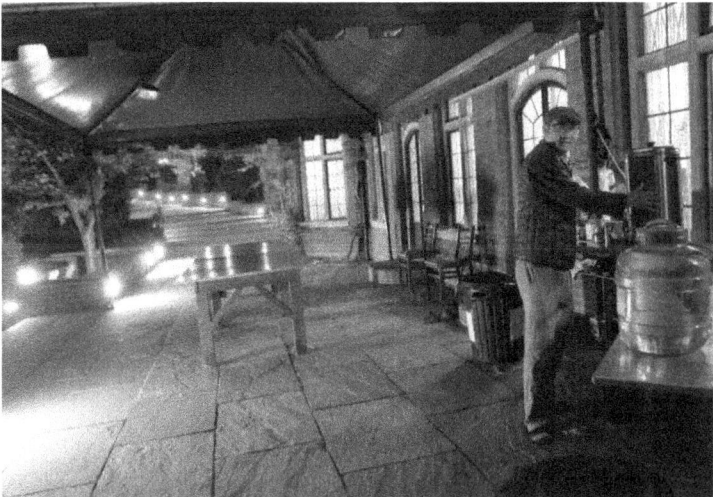

Figure 19.9: The caretaker volunteer, Mr. Kitisak boils hot water

The Buddhapadipa temple has tea and coffee with hot water for the visitors to help themselves to the hot drink. This is a kind of donation, which loving and kind to give food and drink to people when they arrive from the cold weather.

Although the breakfast time for the novice monks are very early. However, the mothers of the novice monks eager to get up early and provide food for her sons. This is the happiest time for her that her son become the novice monks, to learn the Dhamma and he will grow up and be a good person in the future.

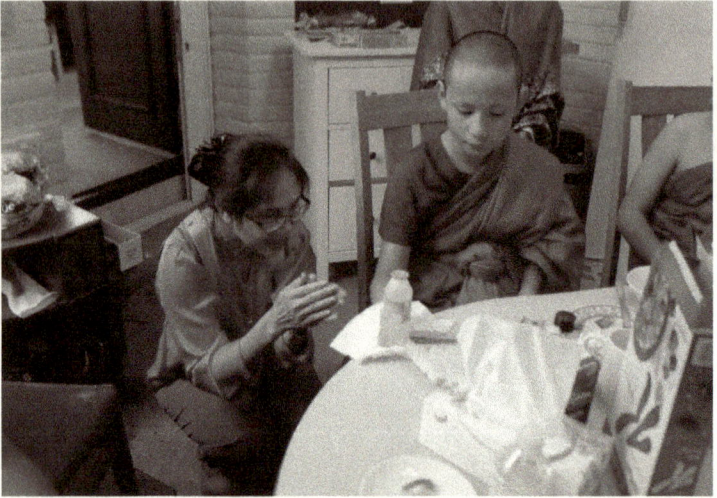

Figure 19.10: Mother of the novice monk offers food

Figure 19.11: The caretaker looks after the novice monks

During the novice monks eating their breakfast, the volunteer caretaker will be there and be available to provide his services. This would help new novice monks to settle and familiar with the monk's system quickly.

Figure 19.12: The teacher and mentor monks, P Nirut

Fortunately, this year there are only four novice monks and all of them get along together very well. They have a head of the novice monks group, who is the eldest to look after the younger ones. In additional, he has a previous experience as a novice monk from last year. Therefore, he knows what would be like and he can give some advice to the new novice monks who have no experience at all.

Also, this would help to assure the new novice monks to get along with the system and every day timetable.

In addition, the teacher monk who acts as their mentor, will be with the novice monks all the time. He is not only looking after them, but also answer questions with a rise regard to be the monk and during their learning to be the good novice monks.

Figure 19.13: The novice monks having their drinks

After the novice monks finish their breakfast, they perform the radiation of love and kindness, which includes to themselves as follows: May I be happy, May I be free from suffering, May I be free from hatred, May I be free from hurtfulness, May I be free from troubles of body and mind, and May I be able to protect my own happiness.

Figure 19.14: Cheeseburger for novice monks

Furthermore, they also radiation their love and kindness to all beings as follows: Whatever being there are, May they be happy, May they be free from suffering, May they be free from hatred, May they be free from hurtfulness, May they be free from troubles of body and mind, and May they be able to protect my own happiness.

Next, the novice monks transference of merit as follows: May this merit accrues to my mother, father, teachers, relatives, friends, supporters, benefactors, gods, hungry ghosts, enemies and all beings; may they be well and happy.

Figure 19.15: Radiation of love and kindness

Finally, they recited the five remembrances as follows: I am of the nature to grow old.There is no way to escape growing old. I am of the nature to have ill health. There is no way to escape having ill health. I am of the nature to die. There is no way to escape death. All that is dear to me and everyone I love are of the nature to change. There is no way to escape being separated from them. My actions are my only true belongings. I cannot escape the consequences of my actions.

CHAPTER 20

Lunch for Novice Monks

Become a novice monk, there is a rule of eating. The monk can eat from the sun rise, but not after lunch time. Therefore, the monk has to finish his food before 12.00 PM. However, the period for people bring food from their home and would arrive at the temple about 11.00 AM.

Figure 20.1: Lunch for the novice monks

Figure 20.2: Lunch for the novice monks

There are separate lunch set between the teacher monks and the novice monks. This is because the monk and the teacher monks have to handle the 227 rules, while the novice monks carry only 10 rules.

There are many things that the monks and teacher monks cannot do or act, for the novice monks they have more freedom than their teacher monks. This may be because the novice monks are still young, need more time to learn. Also, their physical and their body still growing, not as mature as the man's body yet.

Figure 20.3: People offer food to the novice monks

The novice monks have their own dinner table, which they will use for their breakfast and their lunch, including their beverage in the afternoon and in the evening.

The caretaker and people will bring food and put on the table for the novice monks. As they have known that they can eat only the food on the table, they cannot ask for any special food that they like. In addition, they cannot deny the food, which has given to them either.

Figure 20.4: The father of the novice monk offer food

There are a rule and procedure of offering food to the monks and the monks accept food from people. For men, the monks can take food from them directly out of their hand.

However, for women they have to put their yellow handkerchief cloth, where the women will put her food on top of that cloth. This is because the monk status, which is not allowed to have physical contact directly to the women. Also, there is no exception for the monks' mother as well.

Figure 20.5: Reflection on food before eating

Before the novice monks start eating their lunch, they have to perform reflection on food in Pali, which it means the alms food not for fun, not for pleasure, not for fattening, not for beautification, but it is only for the maintenance and nourishment of the body, for keeping it healthy, for helping with the holy life, allay hunger without overeating and continue to live blamelessly.

After the novice monks have their lunch, before they can leave the dinner table, they have to give blessings and transference of merit to people, who give them food to eat. The meaning of blessings is may all distress be dispelled, may all diseases be destroyed, may no dangers be for you, may you be happy, living long, respectful nature, honour in beauty, happiness and strength.

Figure 20.6: Blessings after lunch

It is a routine after the novice monks finish their lunch, they have to give blessings in Pali. They have a meaning as follows: May there be all blessing, may all the Devas protect you well, By the power of all the Buddhas, ever in safety may you be, May there be all blessings, may all the Devas protect you well, By the power of the all the Dhammas, ever in safety may you be, May there be all blessings, may all the Devas protect you well, By the power of all the Sanghas, ever in safety may you be.

CHAPTER 21

Wimbledon Museum Excursion

Figure 21.1: Outdoor education trip

Every Summer Samanera Training Course, the teacher monks will take a group of new novice monk visit the important places around the Buddhapadipa Temple Wimbledon London.

Figure 21.2: Walking trip

On Day 9 after cleaning the temple, feeding the animals in the pond area and have lunch, the novice monks with their two teacher monks have a plan for an outdoor trip, outside the Buddhahapadipa temple.

The best place to visit is the museum around this area, where they can get there on foot, do not have to take a bus or drive a car to be there.

It is a good plan with two adults per four children. Although only one adult is enough to look after these four kids.

Figure 21.3: Walking along the quiet footpath

However, for health and Safety in case there is an emergency, One adult can stay with the group of children, while another one can go and get some help.

They have trips like this every year. Therefore, the teacher monks have some experience and knowledge about what they have to do,how they will get involved, how to control the novice monks when take kids out of the temple area.

Figure 21.4: Pass Gate 9 Entrance for Tennis Players

Figure 21.5: Main entrance for membership

Today they plan to visit the famous Wimbledon Museum. It is about 15-20 minutes walk from he Buddhapadipa Temple. Since most of novice monks live outside the capital of the United Kingdom.

One of them comes from the east of England, one comes from the south of England, one comes from the west and my son comes from the Cambridge area. Thus, it is a good opportunity for them to see the real grass tennis centre court.

Figure 21.6: The Wimbledon Museum ticket counter

The entrance ticket to the Wimbledon museum include the tour to the centre court, which run by tour guides every 15-30 minutes. This tour will open only when there is no tennis match.

Figure 21.7: Lower ground floor display boards

The novice monk not only learn the history of tennis in the United Kingdom, they also see the real tennis rackets from the old model made of wood until the modern technology with fibre. The shape and material of the tennis also change from time to time.

Moreover, the novice monks can see some of the original clothes, shoes and tennis players' uniform, which it has to be white colour both men and women players. It is a traditional since the tennis Wimbledon has established.

To visit the Wimbledon Museum is an educational trip. However, there are many games that they can entertain themselves, and they enjoy challenging their force and speed.

The group of novice monks and their two teacher monks are comfortable wearing yellow robes and walk around the Wimbledon Museum. They do not feel awkward at all with their uniform and they do not feel like they are different from other people who come to visit the museum. Furthermore, they are very polite, quiet, discipline and respect other visitors and following the instruction of the museum's staff.

Figure 21.8: The Wimbledon Museum

Figure 21.9: The Wimbledon games

The interesting part and have a real feeling experience just like we are sitting inside the Wimbledon while the tennis players play the final score before they win the title.

We can feel, hear the sound and see the moving pictures just like the real experience. There are only 10 sets of the head masks build in the individual speakers, this is for the audience to see the 4D real experience.

The novice monks were very excited about the 4D movies. This is their first experience to wear the head mask to watch the animation. They have a good time here in this museum.

Figure 21.10: The 4D tennis Wimble history

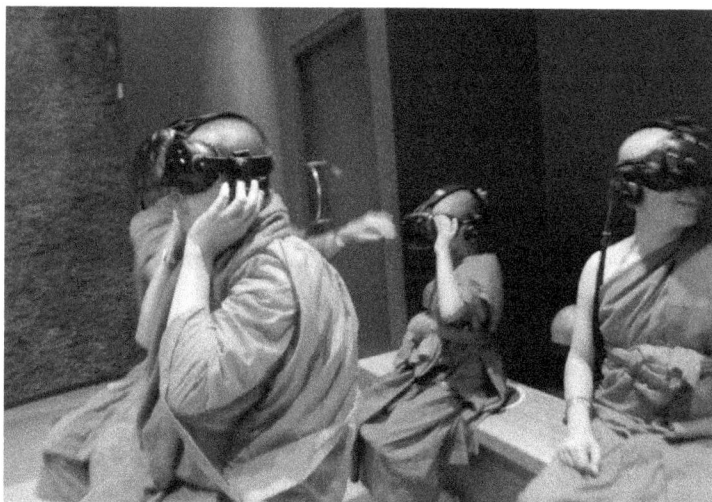

Figure 21.11: The head mask for 4D movie

Figure 21.12: The Novice monk with 4D head mask

The 4D movie shows us some history of the Wimbledon in animation before introducing us to the many courts in the area. The highlight is the final matches for the man single match, the woman single match, the man double match, and the woman double match of the previous year have been shown.

The man and woman tennis Wimbledon trophy have been on shown in the glass cubicle. The novice monks and their teacher monks try to read the winning name for each year. This is one of the highlights of this museum. They are the real trophy that the winners hold them.

Figure 21.13: The Wimbledon winning name

Figure 21.14: The Wimbledon tennis trophy

The tennis winner names were engraved on the surface of the Trophy date back since the first year of the tennis Wimbledon has started.

Some tennis players have their name appear in the Trophy more than one time. Most of them are the world famous tennis players, who play in the big match such as the Australian Open, The US Open and the French Open.

Figure 21.15: Playing games in the Wimbledon Museum

The world tennis match at each tournament are different courts, such as the French open are playing tennis on the clay courts, while the Wimbledon is the grass courts.

After spending a couple hours in the Wimbledon museum, it is time to see the real centre court. This centre court will be for only the important tennis match such as the final match or the famous tennis players match only. The audience has to pay extra prices in order to watch the tennis match in this court.

Figure 21.16: Group photos in front of the Wimbledon Museum

While the group of the novice monks and teacher monks waiting to join the guided tour inside the centre court, they take an opportunity to take some photos as their souvenir with their caretakers, Mr. Kitisak Nuallak.

Figure 21.17: Group photos with caretaker

Figure 21.18: Siting in the centre court at Wimbledon

Figure 21.19: Siting in the centre

The highlight of this outdoor education trip is not only visiting the Wimbledon Museum, but also have a lifetime visiting the centre court, sit on the chair and look at the tennis court, absorb the real atmosphere.

The novice monks learn a lot about the tennis Wimbledon, which it is not famous only from the British people in the United Kingdom, but also the whole world where people travel far away from many countries prior to visit and see the real tennis courts, which they usually watch the tennis matches via the live in their television.

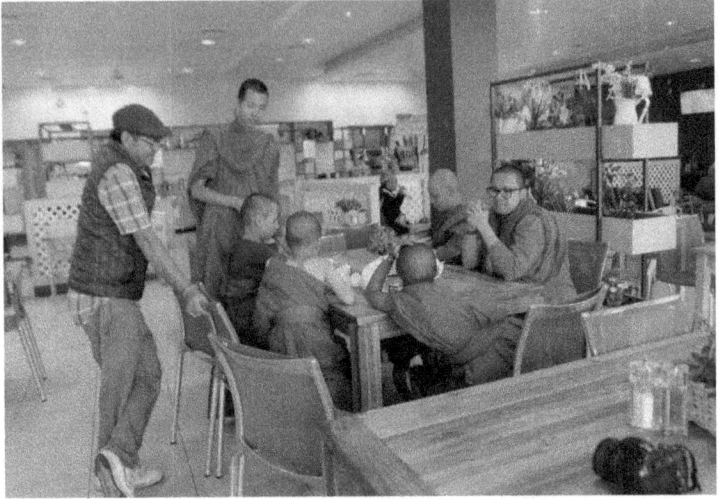

Figure 21.20: Visiting the Wimbledon Café

The Wimbledon trip end at the famous Wimbledon café. The novice monks allow to have some soft drinks, juices and beverage before we start our journey back to the Buddhapadipa Temple on foot. Every person has smiles on their face, especially the novice monks. They enjoy the trip very much. To become a novice monk in UK, do not have to practise meditation all the time.

CHAPTER 22

Wimbledon Park Excursion

In the afternoon on the day six of the novice monks. After they have their lunch and tidy up their bedroom. Their teacher monks take them out to the Wimbledon park.

Figure 22.1: Trip to Wimbledon Park

It is a good sunny day and the weather is pretty warm. All of the novice monks wear their yellow robes open one of their shoulder. However, the teacher monks wear their yellow robes complete, fully dress and cover the whole body.

In practise when the teacher monks go out to the public, he has to dress up fully uniform of the three pieces and cover both arms, both shoulders and whole body.

Figure 22.2: Have fun in the forest

Although the novice monks wear their clothes open one of their shoulders. They still have to carry the biggest third piece on their shoulder. Thus, they will always have it when they want it and it is a part of their clothes uniform.

Figure 22.3: Q & A time with their teacher

A day out into the park to see the nature, the novice monks are very delight and enjoy climbing logs and see some animals. Although they are the novice monks, but they are still a boy, who love fun and running around. They have exploited the woods area.

During the day trip to the park, the novice monks learn the way of the local people live, see the traffic and what is going on in this world.

Life between when they inside the Buddhapadipa temple and their life outside in the real world is completely different. This is the reason that their teachers start to take them out. Thus, they can adjust when they disrobe in the next few days and become normal people, not in the novice monk status any more.

Figure 22.4: Meditation next to the river

After they have a lot of fun, their teacher monks let them practise the sitting meditation by the river bank in the quiet area in the Wimbledon Park.

By the time they finish their meditation practise, it is the time for their beverage.

Figure 22.5: Beverage at the cafe

The beverage time for the teacher monks and the novice monks are between 3.30 PM to 4.30 PM. If they miss the time slot to consume their drinks, they have to skip it and wait until the next beverage time in the evening.

Due to the English weather in summer is very warm and after a lot of walking and playing in the Wimbledon Park, the novice monks are extremely thirsty. Thus, they have drinks and ice cream to cool their body temperature down.

The day out for the novice monks, not only they have some fun playing in the park, but they have learned to practise their meditation in the real environment forest in the mid of the nature.

CHAPTER 23

Basic Dhamma for Novice Monks

Figure 23.1: Dhamma is drawn by P Nirut

The best way to teach and learn basic Dhmama is drawing on the raining day. The weather is pretty wet, it had been raining all day and night.

The basic Dhamma for novice monks was conducted in the novice monk's hut by the teacher and mentor monk, P Nirut. He asked the novice monks to draw some pictures about the Buddha and the Dhamma as their understanding.

Figure 23.2: Drawing of flower lotus

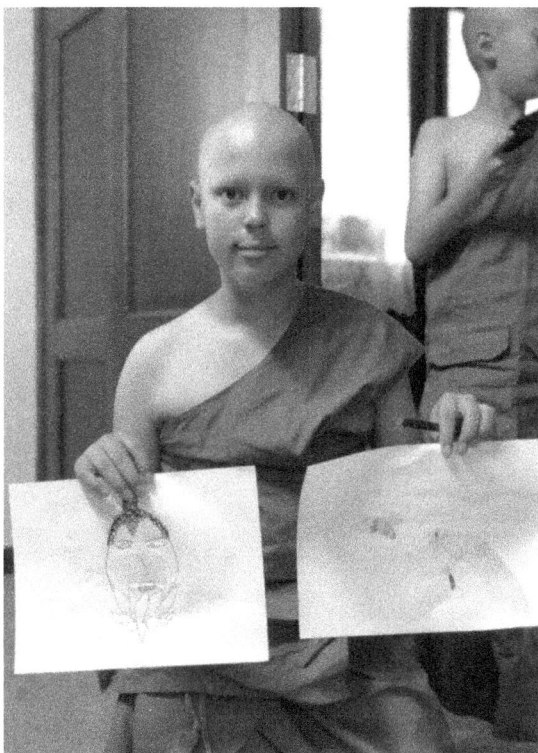

Figure 23.3: Drawing of the Buddha

Some of the novice monks are still too young in order to explain or describe in words about what they understand about the Dhamma in Buddhism. Thus, the easiest way for the children age between 8 -12 years old to emphasis themselves is by drawing and painting.

Some of the novice monks show the picture of the flower lotus, the Buddha head, the Buddha statue and nature.

All of their drawing shows how deeply they understand because the Dhamma is in nature and everything around us. We can see it in every life and in the environment around us too.

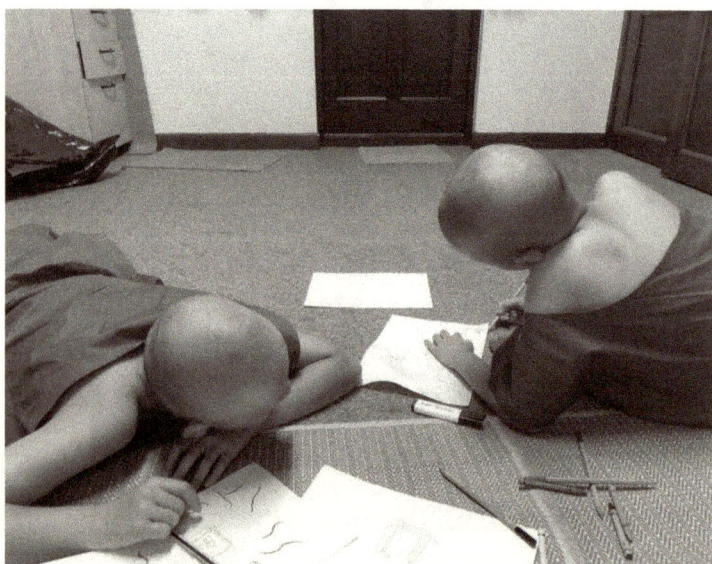

Figure 23.4: Learning Dhamma by drawing

Every novice monks have their own ideas and different from others. The children are quite confident to present their opinion and discuss their reasons behind their drawing.

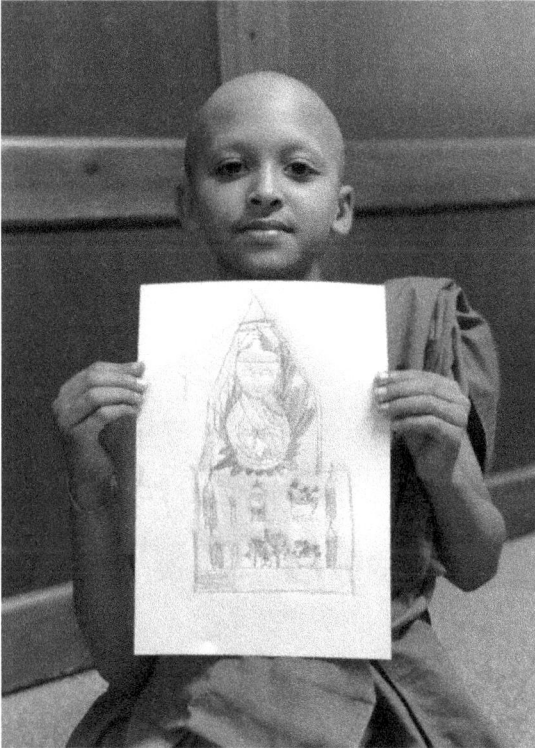

Figure 23.5: Drawing of the Buddha statue

However, at the end of the lesson about the basic Dhamma for novice monks. They have learned about the Dhamma at the level suitable to their age and their knowledge. This may be the first time with this group of the new novice monks to hear a word of "Dhamma" in the Buddhism religion subject.

Fortunately, they are learning while they become the novice monks and learn the Dhamma directly from the teacher monks.

CHAPTER 24

Life of Buddha

Figure 24.1: Learning Life of Buddha

After the novice monks have studied the story of the Buddha of the mural paintings in the Upasatha hall, some of the them just heard about this story for the first time. Some parts of the story are unrealistic and hard to believe. Thus, the novice monks may think it is just a story, not the real story all of them.

The evening class for the novice monks are held between 7.30 PM to 8.00 PM. Before the beverage time.

Tonight their teacher monk, PM Bhatsakorn, prepare some jigsaw materials. The pictures are the story of the Buddha since he was born, grown up, get married, leave the palace, practise many methodologies, become the monk, distribute the knowledge of the Dhamma and life before passing away.

Figure 24.2: Connect the Buddha story

Figure 24.3: Glue the pictures

Each of the novel monk would have different piece and different period of life. The most interesting is they can make it up the story. This children just heard this story once and may be able to recall the whole story in one go.

They are different from the children in Thailand, most kids over there study the Buddha story as the main religion subject. This is because more than half of the people live in Thailand are Buddhists.

In general, education system in the United Kingdom, the religion subject in the primary and secondary school, the students study nearly every religion. Therefore, their knowledge does not in deep as much as the students concentrate on only one religion.

Figure 24.4: Talk about the Buddha story

The teaching method in the Buddahapadipa temple is also different from the way in Thailand. The novice monks in the United Kingdom are familiar and get used to sit on the chairs to study, while the novice monks in Thailand would sit on the floor as well as the teacher monks do too.

Figure 24.5: Discussion about the Buddha story

In addition, the novice monks in the United Kingdom would dare to challenge, discuss, explain their own opinion and ask questions to their teacher monks. They would keep asking the questions until they are clear and really understand the topics. However, there are many times that the teacher monks could not explain why the story of the Buddha is so fantasy more than it would happen with real human.

Become the novice monks in the United Kingdom, they have learned many new things includes the Buddha story, the mural paintings in the Uposatha hall, the many types of the meditation such as sitting, walking and standing.

They told us that they enjoy very much for being the novice monks during the summer training course. They learn a lot and they make new friends. Although they have to get up very early at 5.30 AM, they said it was difficult in the first couple days. However, after they are fine with that. In addition, the early bedtime at 9.30 PM helps them a good long sleep and feel fresh to start a new day and do activities as a good novice monk.

CHAPTER 25

Disrobing Ceremony

Figure 25.1: Disrobing ceremony

The last day of the summer novice monks training course arrived. The schedule of disrobing the novice monks would be set at 2 PM in the afternoon after the teacher monks and the novice monks have their lunch.

There is another purpose that some of the novice monk's parents, their family and friends would like to give food to the novice monks as the last time before they change their status from the monk and become the normal people.

Figure 25.2: Receiving the certificate

Although it is the last day as they are the novice monks, they still have to follow the timetable of the novice monk from getting up at 5.30 AM, have their breakfast before 7.00 AM and attend the morning chanting and practise meditation as usual.

The ceremony starts with the novice monks sit in front of the head of the Buddhapadipa temple and perform the five point prostration three times to pay their respect to the Buddha, the Dhamma and the Songkha. They then ask for permission to resign from the novice monk status to become normal people.

Then, the head of the temple, Phra Thepbhavanamongkol, give each of the novice monk a certification of completion the summer training course from 4th to 12th August 2018.

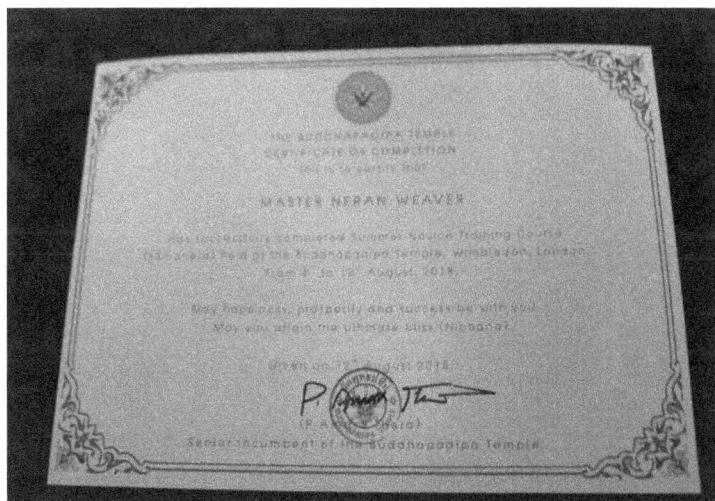

Figure 25.3: Certificate of completion the summer training course

This is a certification of the Buddhapadipa temple, Wimbledon, London. There is a blessing to the Samanera, may happiness, prosperity and success be with you and may you attain the ultimate bliss (Nibbana). The Nibbana is the highest wish level of most of the monks. This is because the Nibbana is the end of human life cycle. This means the person who reaches the Nibbana level, they will be not reborn again. Thus, they do not have to be in the cycle of birth, grow old, ill health, and death

Figure 25.4: Disrobe the yellow robes

The disrobing procedure starts with the head of the temple agree that those four novice monks can resign from their status monks. Then, the head of the temple pulls loose of the yellow robes from the novice monk's shoulder. This means that the novice monks can leave the temple and leave the monk status behind them. Therefore, the novice monks now can change their clothes from the yellow robes into normal clothes.

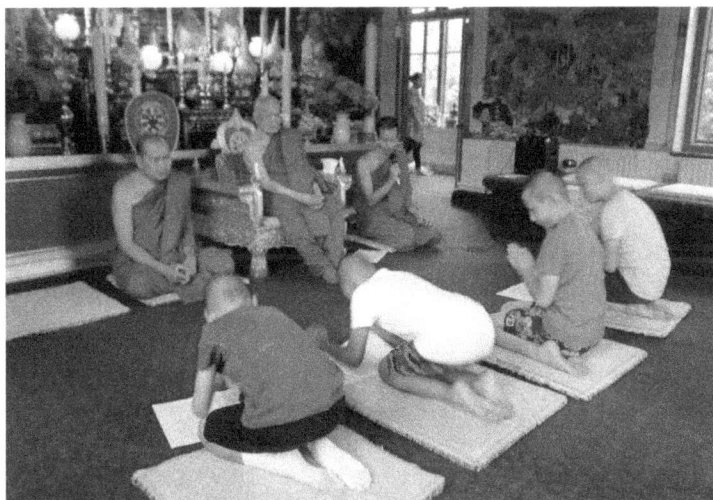

Figure 25.5: Change into casual clothes

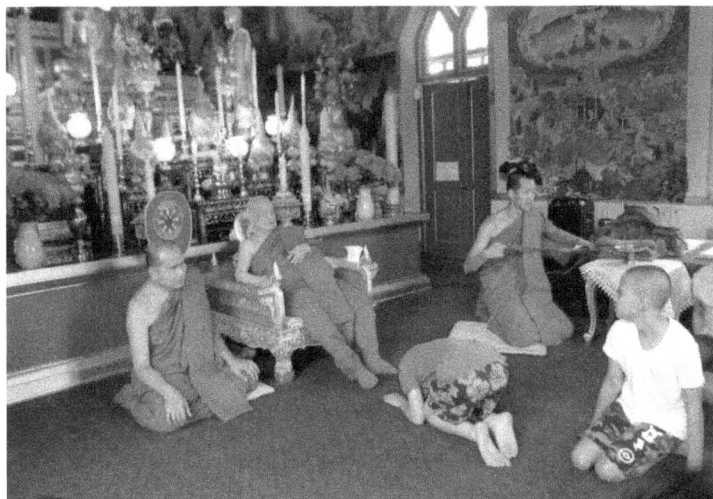

Figure 25.6: Pay respect to the head of the temple, Phra Thepbhavanamongkol

Once they come back as casual clothes, they come to sit in front of the head of the Buddahapadipa temple and their teacher monks again. They performed the five points prostration three times as the last time before they leave the temple, to show their respect to the Buddha, the Dhamma and the Songkha. Now they are free to go.

Figure 25.7: Pay respect to their teacher, P Warapon

Final time, the ex-novice monk perform the five point prostration to pay their respect to the head of the Buddhapadipa, Phra Thepbhavanamongkol, their teacher monk, P Worapon and their mentor teacher monk, P Nirut, as shown in figure 25.6 to 25.8

Figure 25.8: Pay respect to their mentor teacher monk, P Nirut

Figure 25.9: Have a photo with their mentor teacher

Although the ex-novice monks leave the monk status, their relationship between their teacher monks and their mentor teacher monk are very closed. This is because they have lived in this place one day to practise the Pali before they attend the ordination of novice monks and during they were the novice monks. In total, they have lived in this place all day and night for 10 days.

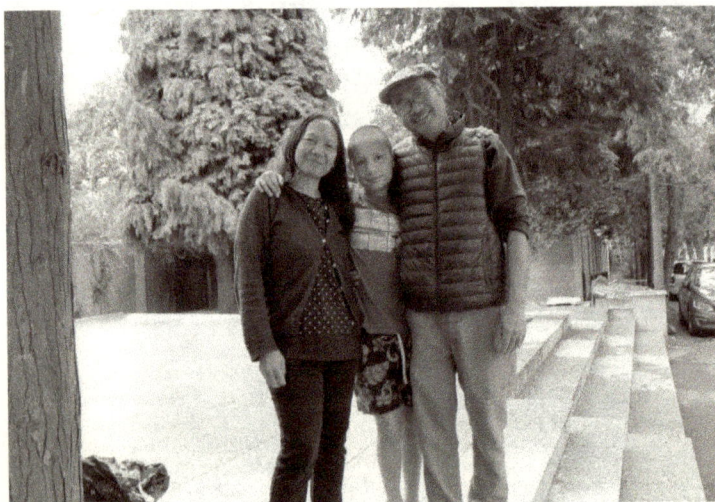

Figure 25.10: The volunteer caretaker

There are one more important people who looked after the group of this novice monks during the summer training course 2018, the volunteer caretakers. They have to get up before the monks and prepare breakfast and lunch for the novice monks. It is a grateful to say a special thank you to them.

The last person the novice monks have to thank is the volunteer photographer, Mr. Patcharaphol Pongvijit, who records the photos whole day on the novice monk ordination ceremony and disrobing ceremony. Some of his photos have been used in this book.

Figure 25.11: The Photographer, Mr. Patcharaphol Pongvijit

Before the ex-novice monk leaves for their home, they donate their money to the Buddhapadipa temple for the gas and electric bill, for repairing the building, for the monk's food and beverage.

Figure 25.12: Donate money to the temple

Figure 25.13: Donate money to the Uposatha hall

Since the Uposatha hall has been built for more than 50 years ago, the roof made of wood in decoration with the Thai paintings, art and architecture, some parts of them were damaged from the cold weather and old age materials.

Therefore, there are in need to repair the building and the roof. However, it needs the specialist Thai artist for this repairing task. This means the temple needs to raise some funding for those repairing. A small donation from the ex-novice monks can help.

When My Son Becomes Novice Monk in United Kingdom

CHAPTER 26

Teacher Monks

Figure 26.1: Phra Thepbhavanamongkol

Figure 26.2: PM Bhatsakorn

Figure 26.3: PM Aphidech

Figure 26.4: PK Sutas

Figure 26.5: P Worapon

Figure 26.6: P Nirut

When My Son Becomes Novice Monk in United Kingdom

REFERENCES

Webpage http://www.padipa.org/

Webpage http://www.watbuddhapadipa.org

PM Bhatsakorn https://youtu.be/_yCyDjqWIAA

When My Son Becomes Novice Monk in United Kingdom